CLEVE WEST

Our Plot

F

FRANCES LINCOLN LIMITED

PUBLISHERS

Frances Lincoln Limited
www.franceslincoln.com

Our Plot
Copyright © Frances Lincoln Limited 2011
Text and photographs other than those listed below
    copyright © Cleve West 2011
Photographs on pages 16 (top left and bottom right),
    17 (top right), 90, 142 © Derek St Romaine
Photographs on pages 17 (top centre), 24, 25, 27 © Christine Eatwell
Drawings and etchings on pages 1, 57, 62 (except top left),
    63 (except bottom left), 75, 80, 129, 185 © Christine Eatwell

First Frances Lincoln edition 2011
This paperback edition 2013

A catalogue record for this book is available from the British Library.

ISBN 978-0-7112-3391-1

Printed and bound in China

9 8 7 6 5 4 3 2 1

Commissioned and edited by Jane Crawley
Designed by Becky Clarke

Sowing times and planting advice are from personal experience
and can vary from region to region. Follow instructions on seed
packets and check with suppliers if necessary.

CONTENTS

By way of a beginning

My first bona-fide gardening experience was the planting of an accidental purchase of Maris Piper potatoes — made even more memorable by unearthing a hibernating tortoise. Running an errand for my mother to buy goods from the DIY store and potatoes for supper, I was delighted to find that our enterprising hardware store sold spuds, saving me a trip to the supermarket. It turned out that I'd bought seed potatoes and I was mercilessly teased by my family until I asked why we couldn't eat them. Were they poisonous? Did they taste awful? No one could give me a straight answer so they were left untouched in the veg rack for several weeks, during which time buds began to appear. Unwittingly (admittedly), I was chitting my first potatoes and it was only out of curiosity that I decided to plant them. The hibernating tortoise, shell-shocked from its undignified wake-up call, was happily reunited with its owner two doors away, although I've often wondered whether the poor creature was actually trying to escape from its owner and all I did was to return it to a lifetime of torture and abuse. I've also wondered whether the tortoise was symbolic, representing the slow start to my career and the fact that it would be seventeen years on a long road into garden design before I would plant potatoes again.

Introducing the plot

Ten years ago, when I proposed writing a book about allotments, the response from publishers was at best lukewarm. 'Allotments are just too traditional,' they said, 'growing food will never set the world on fire and, besides, the American market has no conception of what an allotment is in the first place.'

A year or two later, when books about allotments started appearing on the shelves, I did my best to remain philosophical and, buoyed by the huge groundswell of interest in Grow Your Own, tried again, hoping to focus on the plot I share with my partner, Christine. Still no luck. A personal touch was deemed 'too specialised'. People wanted practical advice on how to grow food and wanted to be told in as many different formats as possible. Again I had missed the boat.

Grow Your Own is no passing fad and may well prove to be the single most important trend in recent gardening history.

Today, as we look more closely into how and where our food is produced, the enthusiasm for Grow Your Own is showing no sign of letting up. Allotments may be yesterday's news but, with increased concern about climate change and 'peak oil' looming on the horizon, Grow Your Own is no passing fad and may well prove to be the single most important trend in recent gardening history.

At last, therefore, I am delighted to have the chance to show how allotment life has affected us and the many others whose lives have been enriched by the simple art of growing food.

But a word of warning. If you've bought this book expecting a definitive guide to growing vegetables, it might disappoint. I'm not saying that there won't be tips and tricks for coercing whatever patch of land you rent to yield sustenance and tastes that will make you feel quite smug at times – I'll certainly share some of what I've learned – but there are a plethora of books and internet sites covering the art of vegetable growing in far more detail, some of which I have given in the list of books. This is the thing: food is only the half of it.

Many have bought into allotments since they became part of the horticultural zeitgeist that seemed to sweep in as the new millennium got under way. But what the books don't tell you is that a large proportion of new allotment tenants give up within a year, overwhelmed by the time needed to keep the plot in good shape. Those that do persevere are often pleasantly surprised to find that allotments are not only about growing food. They are a way of life.

We took on an allotment in the summer of 1999. A daft decision I thought at the time. I was making my way as a garden designer – would my clients still talk to me

Our plot, showing two sheds, raised beds and a climbing frame for beans.

if they ever saw me lugging trug-loads of turnips and cooing over carrots rather than creating sleek terraces, perfect pools and beautiful borders? Besides which, where on earth was I going to find the time?

A couple of friends coerced us into it, in particular one with a tenancy at Bushy Park allotments, not far from Hampton Court Palace. Often referred to as the 'Sleeping Beauty' of all the Royal Parks, Bushy Park had been my childhood playground and was reasonably close to home, but I still needed convincing. When it was explained to me that an allotment might also be useful for storing building materials and plants, I was hooked and within weeks (there was no such thing as a waiting list in those days) we were staring at five rods (126.5 square metres) of couch grass, bindweed and five-foot high brambles.

Faced with the enormity of the task before us, I did what any sensible bloke would do in such a situation. I built a shed. Predictable maybe, but the shed immediately created a hub that would draw us (OK me) to the place in those crucial early months when most people become freaked out by the amount of work that's needed and give up.

Naturally enough our first shed was unconventional. Built largely from reclaimed timber and without a spirit-level, it was immediately christened 'The Wonky Shed' and was surprisingly well received by the existing plot-holders. We soon learned that allotments, for all their conventions and flat-cap connotations, exist as a complex blend of history and tradition where eccentricity is quietly accepted and even expected as par for the course.

While the shed trumpeted our presence as newcomers to the allotment, our first

Metal spheres greet the dawn at one of my projects in Normandy.

The plot being dug over in year two. A friend (Jimmy, standing to the right of the picture) helped prepare the ground for the raised beds.

Slugs. Probably our most difficult adversary when gardening at a distance from home.

year was a disaster in terms of production. One strawberry and a sackful of potatoes was about all there was in an embarrassing harvest. Our naivety in terms of crop protection was woeful. Having disregarded good advice from friendly neighbours, some of whom had been gardening there for over 30 years, we paid the price.

Allotments weren't at all fashionable then and when the council asked us to take on the overgrown plot next door we said yes. We really didn't need it but there were so many slugs holed up in that neighbouring plot that it seemed logical to take it on and create a more organised space. It would also – and here's the real reason I suppose – allow me to build another shed.

In our third season, Ian Hodgson, the editor of the Royal Horticultural Society's *The Garden,* got wind of the fact that I had a plot and asked if I'd be willing to write a series for the magazine. While I felt woefully inadequate in terms of experience and knowledge about vegetable growing, the editor explained that he wanted something from a beginner's point of view. That's exactly what he got and, with my cousin Derek St Romaine taking the photographs, many people in the same situation were able to relate to our experience of fresh food, new friendships and slugs.

As the Grow Your Own movement gathered momentum *Gardens Illustrated* asked me to write a monthly column for them. Again it would be an honest account, relating both the ups and downs of allotment life. Photographer Howard Sooley (another allotment holder) arrived once a month and we'd spend the day at the allotment, enjoying the moment, cooking lunch from whatever was available and resisting any temptation to nip down to the local grocer when things weren't quite as productive as we'd like. By that time I had been pressed into taking on the two plots behind me as well. They were hardly productive, being overgrown with brambles and self-sown trees, but it allowed me space for a third shed (a real potting shed), a social area with a table and seating and my first ever greenhouse.

Today, with more than a decade behind us, we reflect on the joy and revelry our plot has given us and the lasting friendships we have made, bringing home the fact that allotments are as much about the community as about growing food. It is a place for creativity, allowing eccentrics to thrive and all manner of ramshackle to take on a peculiar type of beauty that epitomises allotment culture and the idiosyncrasies we are famous for in the UK. Of course, it can also be frustrating and dispiriting at times when you are at the mercy of matters beyond your control and things don't go to plan, but on balance The Good Life usually has the upper hand.

Over the years ours has evolved into a cohesive, functional space and, for those who still don't really class themselves as experts, reasonably productive. There was obviously some basic design to make the space more practical, but the joy has been feeling our way and being able to garden on a scale that would be impossible in our small town garden.

The only real problem we face is time. Like anyone else in full-time employment, devoting the necessary hours to make the plot as productive as we'd like is always

The editorial team from *Gardens Illustrated* and photographer, Howard Sooley, joining us for lunch.

Christine proudly displaying a mid-summer crop of tomatoes and French beans.

going to be a bone of contention and frustration. Christine (an artist) is someone whose cup is always half full while mine is inevitably half empty, so when things are against us I'm inclined to think about giving up. It passes quickly, usually when I remember just how much work we've put into it and when others visit and tell us just how lucky we are to have a plot in the first place and in such beautiful surroundings. Like anything, if you want something badly enough, you will somehow find the time.

Some people say that allotments and the trend for growing your own food are old hat. Indeed the gardeners' world can be a fickle one but the current groundswell for growing food just gets bigger and bigger and shows no sign of abating. At the time of writing the government had just announced an initiative to sequester land for new allotments in order to reduce the ever-mounting waiting lists. The BP Deepwater Horizon oil disaster in the Gulf of Mexico is another reminder that our ever-increasing global population is placing huge demands on the earth's finite resources. Imagining a world with seriously depleted oil reserves is not for the faint-hearted but it's an issue that many of us will have to face in our lifetime. The ramifications of this are huge and could warrant a book (of not so pleasant reading) on its own; suffice to say that small agrarian communities may once again hold the key to our future survival. The Good Life revolution may be more timely than we realise.

In 2000 I wrote about planting seven fruit trees to mark our commitment. Now, to celebrate our first decade, we've planted eight more, built our fourth shed and an earth oven. There's still much to do. The tenuous sense of ownership we had initially has strengthened a hundredfold despite the fact that we are only tenants. We'll never really own our plot or hand it down to the next generation and there's always the possibility that it will be damaged by vandalism. And, when we've finished with it (or it finishes us), unless it's taken over by someone who has the time and energy to weed, water and outmanoeuvre all manner of things that want to share it, within a year our neglected plot will be unrecognisable. Despite this we, like many vegetable growers throughout the country, have been seduced by the ephemeral nature of our plot. Moving to a house with a bigger garden will always be an attractive notion but for now fresh air, friendship, exercise and the simple pleasure of growing, sharing and eating fresh organic food is, I'm happy to report, as good as it gets.

CHAPTER ONE

Basic principles

I'm a garden designer and Christine is an artist. For us, growing food is a pastime not a necessity and we wouldn't, by any stretch of the imagination, call ourselves vegetable experts. We've learned the slow way, mostly by trial and error, and there are times when we'd rather buy all our food from a supermarket than have to worry about watering, weeding and crop protection. Dr Hessayon's book, *The Vegetable and Herb Expert*, is always on the shed shelf for quick reference but we don't always follow the rules and we find it hard to kill the creatures that try to ruin everything. Things, therefore, don't always go to plan. Tantrums are occasionally thrown. We're nowhere near organized enough to be self-sufficient but 'being there' is just as important as what ends up on the plate. I suppose what I'm really trying to say is that if we can grow vegetables, anyone can.

If we can grow vegetables, anyone can.

From large estates to small balconies the verve for growing food has never been stronger, yet just ten years ago a friend questioned the wisdom of publicising the fact that I had an allotment, saying that the kind of client I was trying to attract would take a dim view of a garden designer getting his hands dirty. I'm proud to say I didn't take heed. Even if my work did suffer, I was happier for it. Today, with allotments and growing food being justifiably *à la mode*, clients are actually asking for veg patches, orchards and forest gardens to be included in the masterplans for their gardens. Some even want to visit our plot and simply hang out.

The frustrating part for us is trying to find quality time to grow vegetables properly. Growing food in our garden at home (if we had the space) would allow us to police our veg patch so much more efficiently than is possible at the allotment, where the journey inevitably makes us disinclined to 'pop-in' for ten minutes weeding or slug collecting. Not always being able to do things at the right time inevitably means that there are disappointments and failures. We're not alone. Allotments are no longer the sole domain of the retired. Many have to tend work and family before making time for their plot and misjudging the number of hours that it takes to keep a plot in reasonably good shape is the reason why many give up within the first year. If this book does nothing other than help people realise that an allotment is a commitment, I'll be happy. It's like keeping a pet, only without all the vet bills.

12th August 2010

Cabin fever. Have been stuck at home for the week after damaging my knee running for a train. Have used the time to knock this book into shape. Think I've broken the back of it. Rain too this week. Lovely. The heavy showers will do wonders for the plot. It will bring the slugs out but I'm past caring now. In any case the ground has been so dry it will save us hours of watering. No consolation for those holidaying in England.

Save for tomatoes in a growbag, Christine and I had little experience of growing vegetables before taking on our plot. Much was learned by trial and error, books, and advice gleaned from existing plot-holders. Of course there were disappointments and failures but, over the years, we have learned from our mistakes. We have also learned that even the mankiest-looking cabbage can provide a hearty meal. An allotment is no place for the squeamish.

Organic principles

My first tentative steps towards making a living in horticulture were taken in the mid-1980s when the notion of organic gardening was itself just finding its feet and people who practised it were generally regarded as bonkers. An elderly aunt needed help with her larger than average garden in West London and – when injury saved me from pursuing a gold medal in the veterans' Olympics – I learned from her and whoever was kind enough to give me advice as I built up a reasonably healthy maintenance round mowing lawns and trimming hedges.

Chemicals were par for the course in those days. It seemed perfectly reasonable to use them at the time and it wasn't until I became a vegetarian that I really began thinking about the food chain and the impact of herbicides and pesticides on the natural landscape. Some temporary work at a salad nursery then opened my eyes to intensive agriculture methods where plastic-lined greenhouses were gas-sterilised twice a year and great vats drip-fed chemical fertiliser into fibreglass modules. Imported solitary bees with miniature hives did the pollinating and when the tomatoes were harvested the whole lot, plastic, fibreglass and hives, were gathered up and buried in an adjacent field. The waste alone was shameful and I didn't buy tomatoes again for ages . . . well, a couple of weeks at least. By the early nineties, when Geoff Hamilton was championing organic methods on *Gardeners' World*, I'd hung up my sprayer and have been gardening organically ever since.

Action shots from my days with Epsom & Ewell Harriers. Today, just looking at these photos make my knees hurt.

Herbicides and pesticides can be used sensibly in private gardens but many people use them in an irresponsible way. Slug pellets are a good example. Just one or two pellets are deadly to slugs and snails yet people commonly use them like mulch without worrying about the birds or hedgehogs they might poison or indeed what chemicals are being leached into the soil. Humans are suckers for short cuts and will usually turn a blind eye when it suits them.

I can't say there aren't times when I wish there was a quicker way of getting rid of bindweed and today I'll admit to having bought my first container of glyphosate for 20 years. I'll probably never use it but bindweed on our plot really has had the upper hand ever since we began gardening there and occasionally one's principles get a little rattled when things look hopeless. Having spoken to organic suppliers over the years it's clear that my good intentions put me on the back foot from the outset. More than one has said that clearing pernicious weeds with Roundup at the start is the only way to give yourself a fighting chance. Often it's impossible to know what the ground has been treated with in the years before (you certainly can't assume it was cultivated organically). Since it takes seven years to attain organic status, it makes sense to start with a clean patch of ground as perennial weeds are virtually impossible to eradicate when they are growing among crops.

4th September 2010

Our third Open Day and once again we are blessed with perfect weather. Three open days is perhaps one too many but there is a healthy turnout to enjoy pasta, pizza and cake. Mary wins the pumpkin competition for the first time despite having spent most of the summer away from home. It's a monster. I will remember the day, though, for an act of stupidity that is almost too embarrassing to put into print. While preparing the fire for the pizza oven I instinctively put my weight on my good leg and tried to break a piece of wood over the thigh of my injured leg. Had it broken, all would have been well. But it didn't and to make things worse I tried again, and again. I thought the pain and the large lump that appeared just above my knee would go away after a few minutes. They didn't. Things got progressively worse until the end of the day when I could barely walk. Back to square one.

Trestle tables buckling under a bumper crop of squash and pumpkins for our open day.

Veggie thoughts

We have been vegetarian for the last 25 years, health and animal welfare being the drivers here, so vegetables are a big part of our life. Lately, while I have let the side down by eating fish from time to time, we have become even more aware of just how much of a drain the meat industry has become on the planet's resources.

A meat diet is twice as expensive as a vegetarian one but when you look at the deforestation, pollution and the CO_2 emissions that the meat industry has caused the cost is much higher. Much of the world's food production is geared towards feeding livestock, and as farming meat requires much more space than vegetables (a third of the world's ice-free land!), it's clear that we could feed many more people in the world with vegetables and in a more sustainable way.

I could go on and give you all sorts of facts and figures (such as it takes 60 pounds of water to produce a pound of potatoes but 20,000 pounds of water to produce a pound of beef) but humans have a habit of switching off when faced with statistics, especially when they challenge their right to eat. I'm not having a holier than thou moment here. I consume the meat industry's subsidiary products – dairy food and leather goods – and am therefore just as complicit as any carnivore. But just a glance at the statistics will show that the world's hunger for meat is unsustainable. What's interesting is that while many people talk of saving the planet[1] and living more

[1] If we have learned nothing else from geologists, we should at least understand that the planet can look after itself. The planet will continue to revolve around the sun for millennia to come. Whether it will be able to support life as we know it is another question and one to which we probably all know the answer.

sustainable lives, most meat-eaters would be loath to give up their Sunday roast or bacon sarnie. We are addicted to meat as we are to oil and economies thrive on it at the expense of the earth's resources.

Biodiversity

Weeds are one thing, bugs are another. Even though the tide is now with organic gardening, some people still have a generally low regard for insects. This is a pity as the food-chain relies heavily on these creatures and makes no distinction between what the gardening press refer to as 'friends' and 'foes'. The late Roger Deakin made an observation about the TV show, *'I'm a Celebrity, Get Me Out of Here!'*, bemoaning entertainment that treats nature as a threat and compounds 'the couch-potato problem by actively alienating Nature'.[2]

With animal welfare being high on our agenda we find it difficult to kill anything in the garden save perhaps

26ᵗʰ September 2010

Our first day here since the open day and still limping. It seems that everything has conspired against us this year to keep us away from the plot. We arrive to find it more overgrown than ever. Jane Crawley, from Frances Lincoln, is coming to see the plot next week so there's an incentive to have a massive tidy up to make a good impression, but there are so many things to do we're at a loss as to where to start. We resort to clearing some of the paths, weeding one or two beds and picking beans, tomatoes and the last of the courgettes. No point in making out that we are in complete control when we're not. That's really not what this book is about.

[2] Roger Deakin's book, *Notes from Walnut Tree Farm*, is refreshingly simple and both poignant and joyous in its individual take on the natural world. It sits by my bed as my bible.

Flowers mix quite happily with vegetables and can attract beneficial insects too.

With 150 species of solitary bees and wasps in nearby Bushy Park, the allotments provide a useful feeding station for many insects.

aphids, which get hosed off rather violently when the ladybirds aren't pulling their weight. A respect for biodiversity and an understanding of the bigger picture is what the allotment has taught us and, at the risk of sounding namby-pamby, airy-fairy New Ageists, the fascination for the way nature works is all part of our enjoyment and fulfilment. That doesn't mean to say that we don't harbour feelings of ill will to these creatures for damaged crops and the enormous amount of time spent relocating slugs and snails to the other side of a stream at the back of our plot. More on slugs and snails later but suffice it to say that they have taken advantage of our live-and-let-live attitude to the point where I have done things that I'm not altogether proud of while writing this book.[3]

Nevertheless, biodiversity is currently the key word in any gardening magazine and no show garden is worth its salt without a nod to it in some way. All good stuff but what's interesting is the way consumers are duped into buying all manner of twee products posing as acceptable (in so far as being aesthetically pleasing) habitats for insects. If there's one thing that insects have learned from being on this earth for millions of years, it's the ability to adapt without worrying about whether their habitats look appealing to humans.

The effects of monocultures and a declining bee population are already being felt across the globe. The USA imports thousands of bee colonies from Australia to help pollinate fruit crops in the west. There are more birds and bees in cities these days than in the countryside because decades of monoculture and spraying have decimated rural habitats. Fortunately, while modern-day agricultural practices and monocultures do pose significant threats to biodiversity, our gardens are actually pretty good at providing all sorts of habitats for many different creatures. In fact before the recent escalation in demand for allotments the government acknowledged the benefits of overgrown plots for biodiversity. It's hard for humans to accept but wildlife actually does quite well without our help, a notion eloquently championed by Ken Thompson in his book *No Nettles Required*. I urge anyone interested in wildlife gardening to read it. If sculptural totems of tubes, crocks and slices of cardboard do nothing else than increase awareness for biodiversity, then I suppose they must be useful, but remember that spiders are just as at home between the lap panels of your shed and solitary bees are happy to hole-up in any suitable dry crevice. They've been doing it for years, long before humans started interfering and aeons before we started to realise just how important they are.

---

[3] The suggestion here is that one's principles get catapulted into oblivion in order to get a book finished but I can assure you that the misdeed in question would have happened anyway, so I might as well do it while writing the book in order to show that some of us do have a breaking point.

LEFT One of the reasons why we don't like using herbicides is that they can harm beneficial insects. ABOVE Growing *Sedum acre* on a shed roof reinstates a planting space that would otherwise be lost.

GM crops

With an ever-increasing population it's logical that we need to find ways to improve food production but people often make the mistaken assumption that genetically modified (GM) crops are more resistant to disease and attack from insects. As far as disease is concerned this may be true. Strains of vegetables selected for their natural resistance to disease can be selected and cross-fertilised to produce a generally more reliable crop with the characteristics of both parents. Resistance to insect attack, however, comes from genetically modifying the crop so that it is either unpalatable to insects or so it can withstand higher doses of pesticide and herbicide. The consequence of this is that vast quantities of insect life (a huge chunk of the food chain) and the related biodiversity will be adversely affected.

Making crops more resistant to herbicides allows weed-suppressing chemicals to be used without harming the crop. The trouble with this, of course, is that the stronger or more frequent doses of chemicals wipe out pretty much everything. They don't just kill aphids and caterpillars but all the good guys as well. The ramifications of this are obvious. Biodiversity is annihilated. The fact too that the herbicides are only supplied by the GM seed companies suggests that the overriding factor here is profit and should set alarm bells ringing across the world. As my grandfather once said, 'There is no shortage of food. The only shortage is of common sense and compassion.'

Sustainability

Perhaps one of the most overused terms in environmental-speak is 'sustainable', and I'm as guilty as anyone else. We aspire to be as sustainable as possible at our plot. We generate our own compost (nowhere near enough for our alluvial soil); we recycle materials; our sheds all have green roofs;[4] I pee in a bucket, urea being a good accelerator for compost and an effective fertiliser for brassicas;[5] we share and exchange food with others at our allotment and occasionally with our neighbours, although we may find it difficult to give away brassicas now they know how we fertilise them.

The downside is that we still use the car to get us there, which to my mind negates any argument that we are cutting out the 'food-miles'. Our plot is a 40 minute walk, a

[4] A green roof simply involves planting a roof space to offset the plant-life and biodiversity that would otherwise be lost to a building's footprint.

[5] It's amazing how many people get squeamish and embarrassed when it comes to sharing their bodily fluids. A number of eminent gardeners have visited the plot and to date none have been at all generous, preferring instead to use the portaloo which, to my mind, is the worse of the two options. At the moment Christine doesn't use the bucket either. She'll hate me for mentioning it and will probably think that the sole purpose of this book is to shame her into action.

15 minute cycle or a 10 minute drive. Invariably the car wins, especially when we plan to cook and there is equipment to carry.

But the road to sustainability is not all that cut and dried. Many of us have poured scorn on the imported food that gives us fruit and veg out of season but are quite happy to pick up a plastic bag of lettuce from the supermarket if we've run out at the plot. Apples from South Africa mean that we can have one a day for the whole year. The amount of energy it takes to keep UK-grown apples in cold storage after they've been picked is comparable to the amount of fuel used to fly them in on planes that are carrying fare-paying passengers and would be coming here anyway.

It's a complicated business and we'll get there one day. It's just taking a little longer than expected.

Health and well-being

Gardening is good exercise and keeps you fit. At least that's what they tell you and, having spent a good deal of my youth involved in personal fitness, I actually feel more qualified talking about this than I do about growing food. Too late. You've already bought the book and, as this is the only chance I'll ever have of putting my sporting achievements into print, let me tell you about track and field athletics. Long jump to be precise.

My personal best was 7.30 metres, that's a squeak short of 24 feet or, if you want to stick to allotment measurements, 1.45152311 rods. That was still quite a way off Bob Beamon's incredible record at the time of 8.90m (set at altitude but nevertheless shattering the dreams of us mere mortals) but I was twice English Schools' Champion,[6] competed for England's under 17 team and was fifth in the UK Championships at Antrim in 1981.[7] I have a dream of making a long-jump themed conceptual garden at the Hampton Court Flower Show in 2012 to coincide with the London Olympics. It will be sublimely simple in design, easy to implement and it will be entitled 'Gold Medal'. Much will depend on whether I still have the enthusiasm or funds for it when the time comes.

Hopeless as a teacher, gardening became an attractive career as I figured it was something that would keep me outdoors and relatively fit – and I'm happy to say it did. As a garden designer, however,

Eating food within hours of it being picked is made even more special if you've grown it yourself.

[6] I am indebted to the great Daley Thompson for not bothering to enter this event and giving us mortals a chance.

[7] Fifth may sound impressive but the competition took place at Antrim during the troubles in Northern Ireland and yes, you've guessed it, only five of us turned up for the event.

In many ways the allotment has become our gym, our meditation teacher and a direct line with the universe.

there's no real call for being energetic except perhaps for flouncing about, waving your arms and pointing at things. Spending all day in an office is the antithesis to what my body needs to feel good about itself and as our garden at home is too small to get physical with, the allotment has played a vital role where health and well-being are concerned.

There isn't any doubt that exercise is good for you, both mentally and physically, and gardening is not only one of the more interesting ways of keeping fit, it can be productive too. It may not be as dynamic and aerobic as running, cycling or swimming but it still gets you out into the fresh air and you're less likely to pull a hamstring or snap your Achilles tendon in the process. A whole day at our plot is occasionally so exhausting that we don't have the energy or inclination to cook the things we have harvested! Our time spent at the plot is therefore valued as much if not more for its therapeutic qualities as it is for providing food.

If you are new to gardening then the best way to injure yourself and dampen your enthusiasm is to go at it hammer and tongs from day one. As I've already said it's a marathon, not a sprint. Little and often is best and small tasks done thoroughly are better than many jobs undertaken in a perfunctory way. A steady rhythm of work will increase the heart rate, improve circulation, tone muscles and keep joints in good order. Light gardening activities, provided none of the above negatives have occurred, can help reduce stress and improve a general sense of well-being.

Sanctuary

Unless you suffer from agoraphobia, space is invigorating, stimulating and relaxing. Without the boundaries we have in our private gardens, allotments give you sunrise, sunset, stars and a place to really appreciate the seasons. Opening and closing the large wooden gate to the allotment is therapy in itself.[8] The rattle of chain and familiar squeak has, over the years, induced an almost Pavlovian conditioning so that even the imagined sound can take you to a different world in an instant. Increasingly it has become a place to wind down, escape and do our own thing, a bit like a holiday home or beach hut, except with less loafing about in slippers or swimwear.[9]

It's not something that I dwell on but occasionally I wonder about the need for sanctuary. Our garden at home serves very well as a retreat. Evergreen, intimate and with water and minimal maintenance, this alone is more than enough to suffice in terms of relaxation. The allotment, with all the work, organisation and protection it involves, is often exhausting, frustrating and annoying, so why it should still provide a sense of refuge seems strange. I suspect the dynamics of an allotment suit people who are not inclined to sit about but always have to be doing something. The combination of getting good exercise while nurturing plants and producing something that you can eat at the end of it is nourishing on many different levels.

Bushy Park, just over the fence from our plot, accentuates the feeling of sanctuary.

---

[8] Provided, of course, that the moment isn't spoiled by some foul-smelling waste dumped in the bin nearby.

[9] It's worth pointing out that allotments are known havens for eccentrics and if you were inclined to walk about in flippers, trunks, snorkel and mask there's less likelihood of someone phoning for an ambulance than if you did the same thing in the local high street.

CLOCKWISE FROM TOP Entering the allotment from a busy road is like being transported into another world; squash harvest; young pea pods; harvesting rhubarb, 'Coutts Red Stick'.

CHAPTER TWO

People

While growing food was our main reason for taking on the plot, the people on the allotments are a big part of the picture too. This may sound completely naïve and perhaps a little self-centred, but it's something I hadn't fully grasped until we'd seen through our first few seasons.

I suppose I didn't know what to expect when we first started clearing our plot but I imagined allotment folk to be quiet, reserved and perhaps even a little odd. I thought of the film *The Wicker Man*, where Edward Woodward's lukewarm reception from uncooperative residents of a Scottish isle set the pace for ensuing weirdness and terror. But most of the plot-holders we met in that first year turned out to be a friendly bunch; helpful too as they tried to gauge whether our enthusiasm was genuine or a cover for the fact that we had absolutely no clue when it came to growing veg. The older stalwarts (most of them men in those days as allotment fervour hadn't quite kicked in) were more than generous with advice. But behind the smiles, encouragement and occasional teasing it was clear that they saw us as temps – good for a season – two at the most. It wasn't until I'd planted fruit trees at the end of our second year that we were taken a bit more seriously and I could sense the nods of approval as seven maiden apples and pears were planted as a symbolic mark of commitment.

Some of the things you are being told may turn out to be pearls of wisdom.

If I'd been more sociable at the outset, I would probably have made fewer mistakes but I enjoy the solitude of gardening, it's what drew me to it as a career; the repetition and rhythm of digging, pruning and watering I find both meditative and therapeutic. The allotment, just a step away from communal gardening, turned out to be challenging in a way I hadn't expected. People talked. Not only that but some people liked to talk quite a bit. Hardly surprising really as most were retired but it still came as a shock and, if I'm honest, a little intrusive. There are also one or two who have that particularly annoying habit of not being able to gauge when the conversation has ended. A natural pause or an embarrassed silence followed by a deep breath from me and 'Right, well I'd better get on' seems to offer little or no clue. I can only put it down to deafness and suspect that if I stay there long enough I too will, one day, be doing exactly the same to some unsuspecting newcomers anxious to make use of the little time they have to tend their plot. You have to realise that this is part of the deal and learn to keep moving while talking if you are to get any work done at all. You also have to understand that some of the things you are being told may turn out to be pearls of wisdom. I often wish that

David wielding a two-gallon watering can. He and his wife Julie have often helped us out with watering tasks when we've been away for any length of time.

Some people become an intrinsic part of your life, whether or not you socialise with them outside the plot. CLOCKWISE FROM TOP LEFT David; Mary; Mrs Luu and her prizewinning pumpkin; Su with a basket of bitter melon; Sainsbury's John; Giuseppe and his hens; Len; Julie.

I'd listened a bit more closely to the advice that was being freely offered instead of worrying that time was being wasted through idle chit-chat.

For example Len, one of our longest-standing plot-holders, told me several times to cover my brassicas to keep the pigeons at bay. I didn't see the point. Mine had been uncovered for several weeks without any damage, so I ignored his advice, only to find most of them ripped to shreds the following week. Sheepishly I covered the few that had somehow been spared the assault.

2nd August 2009

Poor Sainsbury's John has had to go home to change his trousers after they caught fire in his shed. Henry explains that ash from John's cigarette had dropped into his lap and smouldered for a while before his cords started smoking. I don't think there were flames but he had to put himself out with water, which then made it look as though he'd wet himself. I ask Henry why he didn't offer to help. He says that 'a man's privates, be they on fire or not, are his own business'.

Many months later, when there was still no sign of any florets, I convinced myself I'd grown a duff batch and, in an attempt to avert even more ridicule, I yanked them up for the compost heap. I don't blush easily but when Len enquired as to why I had pulled up the broccoli just when they were about to set their florets I struggled to make up a credible reason. Of course there was no point, I simply had to admit that I hadn't read the instructions. Much of the laughter coming from the mid-morning coffee break was almost certainly directed at me that day so I took it on the chin and reminded myself that I was a designer, not an expert in growing food, and from now on would willingly take advice whenever it was offered.

RIGHT Open day means fresh pizza, onion bhajees and plenty of cake.

As the years went by and allotments hit the gardening headlines, new faces began to appear. With 385 plots at Bushy Park there were plenty available (I had almost 20 rods and was still being offered more by the council) and, in a way, this helped to galvanise our own resolve to develop our plot as a way of life and not just something to play with when the sun came out. With families now taking on plots the dynamics were changing. Grow Your Own was attracting a younger audience. This was generally good news but as some of the more elderly plot-holders either moved or passed on I began to see just how valuable they were and the knowledge that was disappearing with them. Like anything in life, a mixture of old and new helps keep a place alive and vital.

The dynamics of allotments depend on variety. Not just in terms of vegetables, methods or eclectic styles but in the characters that inhabit them. Each person has their own idiosyncratic ways and peculiarities. Colour, religion, politics, dress sense (not to mention levels of nakedness), efficiency, ability, sociability, transport, sheds, fruit cages, bird feeders, scarecrows, veg varieties, veg to flower ratios, killing methods, compost heaps, bonfires, generosity, organics, DIY or off-the-shelf, maverick or by-the-book, labeller or non-labeller, bull-shitter or diffident, cooperative or pain in the arse, barking mad or ever so slightly mad (because you have to be a little touched to have an allotment) . . . everyone, praise the Lord, is different.

No longer are allotments in the sole ownership of the solitary working-class man who, apart from getting away from ''er indoors', did actually subsidise the family's

Saturday 17th July 2010

Open day. A beautiful sunny day, not too hot. Coinciding with the first ever Hampton Hill Summer Festival, Giuseppe and I are cooking and I arrive early to fire up the earth oven. I'm aghast to learn that Henry has decided to work for most of the day. I quickly call him and the panic in my voice must have unsettled him, as not only was he back by mid-morning he also dug up his whole beetroot crop for the veg stall. His 'ladies' have also excelled themselves with cake. There's a whole table of it and two boxes of the best cup-cakes (I'm not a fan of these) I have ever seen or eaten.

Ted arrives too and goes way beyond the call of duty in supplying a whole table full of vegetables. I covet my veg too much to be so generous.

By 11.30 we were producing the best pizza Bushy Park allotments had ever seen in its 120 year history. I can say this because it has Giuseppe's seal of approval. He declares it the best pizza he has eaten in England. Giuseppe is a chef from Naples so I have every right to feel a little smug, although Jamie Oliver's pizza dough recipe and the earth oven should take the lion's share of the credit here.

Julie takes over when the gates open at 12.30 to allow me to cook onion bhajees in my new kuri. She can't cook the pizza quickly enough and slices are being taken from the peel before it even gets to the table where all the food is being served.

Cooking in the new, much larger kuri is luxury. I can cook batches of fifteen at a time so don't feel quite so under pressure when a queue starts to form.

Ray Brodie, Bushy Park's manager, comes to check that all is OK. Despite his protestations about having had a good lunch, I still managed to tempt him with two bhajees.

Overall a successful day. Many visitors had never seen inside the allotment walls. The highlight was probably the elderly gent in a wheelchair who came onto our plot with his carer drawn to the smell of cooking coming from the pizza oven. He said he didn't care for pizza but Christine tempted him to try a slice. He liked it so much he got out of his wheelchair to kiss all the women on the plot before departing, saying it had made his day. I guess some people will eat anything for a kiss.

It has become something of a necessity to spend at least as much time eating at the plot as weeding.

food bill. You only need to see the cars at allotments these days to see that things have changed. Today allotments are just as fashionable among the middle classes and women. This may seem a shame, an abhorrence even, to those who have known allotments since the dark days of World War Two but, in many respects, it has levelled the playing field and booted any notion of horticultural snobbery firmly into touch.

Allotment folk are, on the whole, pleasant and amiable because gardening does seem to bring out the best in people. With 385 plots there is a broad slice of the local community and, while there will be differences of opinion and personality clashes along the way, the suggestion is that allotments are as close as you might get to an utopian society. In reality, the internal politics mean that allotment people are really no different from any other community, it's just that there's more scope for eccentricity. Why no one has written a successful sitcom about allotments is completely baffling.[1]

Most of us get on most of the time. Some, of course, don't. Disputes aren't uncommon and, on rare occasions, the council has had to step in to calm things down, but that's life, albeit represented in a microcosm of veg, weeds and tinpot sheds. The interesting thing is that allotment holders rarely meet socially outside the plot. Of course you'd acknowledge someone if you passed them in the street but seeing them out of context, doing normal things, is always a bit peculiar. I think it's because there's always so much to do at the allotment that the notion of anyone having a life outside is just very difficult to imagine.

[1] I can say with some authority that sitcoms have been written about allotments because I've co-written one (predictably entitled 'Losing the Plot') with a friend who has an allotment in Tolworth. Needless to say (like all the others referred to in our rejection letter), it wasn't considered good enough, but it's only a matter of time before someone taps into allotments as a rich source of comedy gold.

Chi

Some people hide from Chi. He has a habit of stopping to tell you just what you should be doing to make life easier for yourself. Not in a know-all sort of way. He just can't bear seeing people wasting energy. The way he works with his Vietnamese family is an inspiration to many of us in terms of just how productive a plot can be. From tilling to trimming they are often seen working as a family unit and are a lesson in cooperation and efficiency. The rate at which Chi can clear a plot with his adze (a large spade-like blade but used like a mattock or pickaxe) made our efforts with a spade look embarrassing by comparison and eventually I took enough note to buy one for myself. My back has thanked me for that ever since. Chi and his family grow a fascinating range of oriental vegetables and, until this year, have won the prize for the biggest pumpkin for as long as I can remember.

Dhundi

I met Dhundi shortly after we acquired our plot. He and his wife Natasha were expecting their first baby and he barely spoke a word of English, having left his native Nepal some months earlier. He worked for me doing garden maintenance for a few years before joining a landscape contractor. Within six years he was speaking fluent English and formed his own landscape company and is now on my preferred list of contractors for the gardens I design.

Apart from encouraging us to grow various types of karella, bottle gourds and other Asian vegetables, Dhundi's enthusiasm for cooking at the allotment fired our imagination. It changed the way we used the plot to a point where it became more of a weekend retreat than an onerous chore.

Sadly for us, he and his family have now moved to Dorset and, while he still works with me on landscape projects, we don't have the pleasure of seeing the children grow up.

Giuseppe

Despite the fact that he started his allotment around the same time we did, we've only really got to know Giuseppe over the last year or two. Like us he enjoys the solitude of gardening and, happy with his own company, largely keeps himself to himself. A chef (originally from Naples) by trade, Giuseppe has also made a big effort to breathe life into the allotment shop after a period of inactivity and we have joined forces to improve the choice of food offered on open days. He keeps chickens rescued from battery farms and neighbouring plot-holders share the responsibility, highlighting the cooperative potential of allotments.

Henry

The first person that newcomers are likely to meet at the plot. This ruddy Glaswegian, in khaki fatigues and with hair more tousled than a windswept Straw Peter, is the living incarnation of The Green Man. He has a heart of gold, looking out for the vulnerable and helping many newcomers get started at the plot. For good or ill, he'll speak his mind and has contributed the most to the allotment by way of working behind the

Just a few of the characters we know at our plot.

scenes to create an atmosphere of fair play and cooperation. He can talk for Scotland but exists as the common denominator at the plot and is always around to give us the lowdown on what's afoot. If you need a shed or greenhouse, chances are that Henry will source one for you, often liaising between parties and even fetching and erecting for no profit, which, in my book, goes way beyond the call of duty. He's thick-skinned enough for me to be brutally honest about him on these pages (pages he has badgered me to write for almost ten years) but he might get upset if I say that he's also one of the most sensitive flowers on the plot, which is quite endearing. His eccentric ways can be a bit too much for conservative types and I suspect they wouldn't miss him if he left. Christine and I would though. We'd miss him a lot.

Julie and David

Some of the first friends we made at the plot. They are rare in that they are the only couple we socialise with outside the allotment walls. American-born, Julie is the driving force behind the actual food-growing. She has the greenest fingers I know and can usually supply seedlings of pretty much anything should we forget to sow or get our first batch of something munched by slugs. David does much of the preparation and erecting of structures but is easily distracted by coffee vapour on a south-westerly breeze from our plot. Julie has inspired us to take advantage of cooking at the plot and has her own repertoire of recipes from Boston Beans (see page 156) to banana cake to keep everyone happy on open days. Suppers at the plot with these two have lasted well into the early hours.

Mary

Mary wears some of the best knitted jumpers ever seen at Bushy Park allotments. She may be retired but she's also a grafter, often working long hours not only on her own plot but also for others who can't manage theirs for whatever reason. At her age (and I'm too embarrassed to ask her), that's no mean feat. She's always around to open and close the greenhouse when we're not there and on open days she'll man the stands for hours, whatever the weather. Many think that she deserves a community action award until she spoils things by thoughtlessly going to Ireland once a year to see her family. Shocking behaviour.

Phil

An engineer's mind at the plot is always a useful thing. Who else would document sowing and harvesting dates with records of yields of not only what he's grown himself but also what he's been given by other plot-holders? His plot is slightly smaller than ours but his clever use of space means that he is far more successful than most in terms of variety of produce and quantity. The data he's collected over the last few years warrant a book of their own. At the time of writing, Phil has just taken over as chairman of the Bushy Park Allotment Association's committee. Those who know him feel that we are entering a golden age at the plot.

Rick

Every so often, mostly during the summer months, a horn will ring out across Bushy Park allotments. This is Rick flying a flag for eccentricity by blowing into anything tubular that comes to hand, mostly watering cans. Blasts vary in pitch according to the size of the receptacle and how much water is in it. The note from a small Haws can might attract the local hunt (if one existed), while the deep groan from a two-gallon French watering can should have the Stewards of Gondor preparing for battle. I joined in for several weekends, sounding a range of cans around midday hoping it would catch on. It didn't. Most people just shook their heads and looked away, clearly embarrassed. (I'm not sure whether describing someone as eccentric is rude or not but I'm hoping Rick will take it as the compliment it's meant to be.)

Sainsbury's John

So called because he works at Sainsbury's and his name is John. He's had a plot for eight years and, like Henry, does a lot of work behind the scenes, including charity work for local schools. Shift-work means that John occasionally gets two or three days on the trot at the plot where he's completely in his element. He sees the positive in everything (a useful trait to have at an allotment) and made an earth oven for himself when the rest of us were moaning about clay messing the place up when a new water main was installed.

As a comic duo, Sainsbury's John and Henry are a sitcom waiting to happen.

Ted

Ted works 20 rods next door to Phil. He has been coming to Bushy Park allotments since 1960 and is therefore one of the longest-standing tenants. A touch deaf, conversations with Ted can be very frustrating at times and his bonfires smelling of old socks are legendary. He grows so much food that he spends half his time giving it away, a generosity of spirit that makes allotments what they are. Some of the vegetables he grows he doesn't even like himself. 'I just do it for the fun of it.' Having been at the plot for such a long time, he knows just how tired the soil can get and pays particular attention to composting and watering. Many a time has he rescued us with 'spares' from his plot when our seedlings have taken a hiding from pigeons or slugs.

Mum with my cousin and photographer, Derek St Romaine.

CHAPTER THREE

Methods

T he notion of growing your own food is extremely attractive and for some it really is the 'The Good Life'. What many fail to grasp, however (I know I'm repeating myself here but it's a point worth driving home), is the amount of time and effort it takes to keep a plot in good order and productive. Computers, mobile phones and other devices were, as far as I recall, meant to make things easier, keep us organised and free-up time for more leisurely pursuits but, somehow, most of us seem to have less time on our hands than we did before the new technology came into being. A little discipline is invaluable if you are thinking of taking on a vegetable plot for the first time.

A little discipline is invaluable if you are thinking of taking on a vegetable plot for the first time.

The sooner you can understand that growing food is a marathon not a sprint the better. OK that's a bad analogy; the only good part of a marathon is the finish but I'm sure you get my drift. Lia Leendertz's book *The Half-Hour Allotment* is perfect if you need to regulate your time at the allotment in the most efficient way. I'm more of a dreamer and could easily spend half an hour admiring the pattern on a snail's shell, but the book encourages you to have a clear idea of what you are going to do *before* you get there so you can concentrate on the tasks that need doing and then, if there's time, rescue hypothermic bees later. [1]

Choosing the plot/analysing the site

Perhaps the most important part of the commitment to an allotment is choosing a site that is relatively close to home. Within walking or cycling distance is preferable. Certainly no more than 15 minutes' drive away. Then there's the plot itself. With allotments being so scarce these days most people don't have the luxury of choice, but it's worth finding out what you can beforehand just to know what might be in store. Good access, a convenient water supply and an existing shed are the main attractions for newcomers. Perennial crops such as rhubarb or other inheritances such as fruit trees and bushes can also be a bonus. We chose ours primarily because it was next door to a friend, had space to park the car and was close to a mains tap. What we didn't take into account was that

Sweetcorn being grown in 9cm pots to give them a better chance against slugs.

[1] Bees occasionally get stranded at dusk, especially in spring when temperatures can fluctuate wildly. They can be revived and if you're gentle there's little danger of being stung. Cupping a bee in your hands and breathing on it is often enough to get it flying again (be careful not to open your mouth too wide) but some need feeding with a drop of sugar solution to find the energy to fly. While a little time-consuming, getting a bee airborne again is one of those small deeds that can make you feel all warm and cosy inside for the rest of the day.

the plot loses light in late afternoon, quite a disadvantage in many respects. Neither did we check properly to see what weeds we might inherit and, as it turned out, we inherited what might be a national collection of pernicious weeds.

Try and look at a prospective plot during the summer so you can see exactly what weeds might be growing. Annual weeds are no problem; a hoe can deal with those. Couch grass, ground elder, bindweed (convolvulus) or mare's tail, however, are the worst sort of weeds to have to deal with and will involve much work if you are to get rid of them. You'd be very unlucky to encounter Japanese knotweed on an allotment as this weed is outlawed and there are severe restrictions on how to deal with it. If you see it anywhere near the plot you are considering, do yourself a favour, turn around and go home. Our plot had, and still has, couch grass, bindweed and brambles. Brambles are a bit of an effort to get out (a mattock is the best tool for grubbing them out) but they do do quite a good job of shading the ground and preventing other weeds from getting established. Couch grass and bindweed take much longer to eradicate. Our plot is never free of them and, as I've already mentioned, a bottle of glyphosate is in my shed . . . just in case. Using it now will be fiddly to say the least, as bindweed has evolved to grow in the most obscure places and is more than happy to share root space with your favourite plants. I suppose that makes it nothing less than a terrorist working on the assumption that we wouldn't risk harming its hostages to get rid of it. A shame really as it has one of the most beguiling flowers going. A friend told me that the best time to apply the weedkiller is on a dry day in late summer. As you may have guessed, I am no expert when it comes to applying chemicals so can offer no advice apart from suggesting that you should read the instructions on the packet.

Design

Once you have chosen your plot it's a good idea to take a little time to consider its design. 'DESIGN!!!???' I hear you say. 'What on earth has growing food got to do with design?' The answer to that, of course, is 'everything'. How you arrange your plot, whether you draw it on paper or not, is design. You are arranging space either logically, intuitively or creatively to get the best from it in terms of production or aesthetics and occasionally both. Some people think that the word 'design' is a little too pretentious and would rather their garden 'evolve' over the years so that, by trial and error, its character and that of the owner are revealed in a natural progression. However you like to describe the process, it is still design. You are still working things out, placing elements, plants and hard landscaping in a rational, coherent way to improve ergonomics and the practicality of a space; it just takes much longer to see the results. Whether your ideas are successful, pleasing or productive is another matter but, whether you are conscious of it or not, design will have some say in the matter.

Traditionally, vegetables in walled gardens and allotments are grown in rows or blocks carefully arranged so that taller crops don't cast too much shade on smaller ones. Every bit of soil is planted to maximise yield and paths of compact soil provide access for planting, weeding and picking. When we realised the enormity of what we had taken on, we decided very quickly that raised beds were the answer. Aesthetically

Raised beds under construction with landscape fabric being used to stop weeds growing on the paths.

pleasing and useful for keeping a record for crop rotation, their main purpose, for us at least, was psychological in that being able to weed one bed in an hour or so gave us a semblance of control.

What we didn't bank on was that the paths between the raised beds require a fair bit of weeding themselves and that the timber boards used to raise the soil eventually rot, creating the perfect habitat for slugs and snails to hide and lay their eggs. As the boards decay we've been disinclined to replace them and, for now, will make do with the mounds of soil. We've even talked of getting rid of the paths altogether as the woodchip that we've used each year as a surface has rotted down to make a fine growing medium. Talking is one thing; removing the one and only device that gives us a vague notion that we are in control might be just plain daft. I think we'll stick with design.

If you are thinking about creating a new vegetable plot in your own garden or like the sound of raised beds, then think about making a simple survey of your patch of land and playing about with some shapes. Drawing on graph paper will make things easier in terms of getting the scale right. Centimetre squares can represent a metre (1:100) or half a metre (1:50) and will enable you to mark your space out accurately with a few basic measurements. If you don't fancy yourself as a draftsman, paper or card can be cut into squares and rectangles and arranged until you get the composition right. A metre-wide path will allow room for a wheelbarrow; half a metre is still sufficient for walking on where space is tight. Vegetable beds at 1.25m wide allow you to reach into the centre from both sides and save you from walking on the soil. Of course, you may prefer an elaborate design for a vegetable garden but, unless you're opening your garden to the public or have ideas of grandeur, it's best to keep things as simple and practical as possible.

OVERLEAF Our plot in spring looking reasonably tidy and ready for a new season. In the background (from left to right) the tool shed, the Wonky Shed, the greenhouse and the summerhouse in the neighbouring community orchard.

Dig or no dig

With pernicious weeds having the upper hand at our plot, we dig in order to keep a semblance of control. A more thorough initial clearance would have allowed me to adopt a no-dig approach, a system that makes so much sense in terms of letting worms and invertebrates do much of the work by aerating and fertilising the soil while leaving its structure intact.[2]

Old school methods tell you that digging opens up the soil and provides an easier ride for plant roots, especially the long tap-roots of carrots and parsnips. A carrot I once found growing quite happily in a crack on a terrace suggests that this simply isn't true.

A year or two of adopting the no-dig method saw the bindweed proliferate to the point where I would have been happy to napalm the whole site and, as I write, I'm looking a bottle of glyphosate in the eye for the first time in 20 years. The guilt associated with this purchase is enormous for someone who has practised (and occasionally preached) organic methods for most of his gardening career, but I feel I am at my wits' end and have more or less given up hope of ever ridding our plot of convolvulus. As a last-ditch attempt to make this course of action completely unnecessary I have taken to spending two hours at the allotment every other morning hand-digging the worst areas. The exercise is good, the solitude welcome and the privilege of greeting some frosty dawns has been magical but I know that, no matter how diligent I am in picking out every last bit of white root, it will be back.

Apart from appealing to the lazy in me, no-dig gardening would not only save time but also alleviate the water loss from our alluvial soil. Our sandy loam is typical of many gardens that are less than a mile from the River Thames. To its credit the soil is free-draining, easy to dig and quick to warm in spring, but it does need more watering during a drought and nutrients leach from it more freely. Digging causes moisture in the soil to evaporate more quickly and nutrients are lost through damaging the soil's structure. The no-dig method emphasises the importance of mulching the soil with compost during winter to help suppress weeds and retain moisture while allowing bacteria and invertebrates that live in the soil to process the nutrients, making them readily available for plants.

Fertilisers

There is a lot of fuss made about soil fertility, sometimes too much. Of course we should be concerned with the health of our soil, especially when it's used intensively for food production, but many people go overboard with artificial fertilisers to a point where it can be detrimental to the soil's natural balance, not to mention our natural waterways.

If you are thinking about using artificial fertilisers it's worth understanding the N-P-K ratios just so you know what you're putting on the soil. The letters N-P-K are usually found on the bag or packet and indicate the three basic elements required for healthy plant growth: nitrogen (N), phosphorus (P) and potassium, which is also referred to as potash (K). Growmore, a typical general fertiliser, has an N-P-K

---

[2] Charles Dowding's excellent *Organic Gardening: The Natural No-Dig Way* is easily one of the best books on vegetable growing on the market.

Organic farming uses approximately 26 per cent less energy to produce the same amount of food as non-organic farming.

ratio of 7-7-7, indicating that it contains 7 per cent of each element. Homemade compost will have something like 5-5-5.

Nitrogen (N) promotes leaf growth, making plants grow faster and greener, phosphorus (P) is important for seed germination and root development, and potassium (K) for flower and fruit development, not to mention disease and drought resistance. Fertilisers with a higher nitrogen content (e.g. 12-7-7) are higher in nitrogen and therefore more beneficial to leaf vegetables and lawns. Fertilisers with a ratio of 7-12-7, indicating a higher percentage of phosphorous, will benefit root crops while high potash feeds (e.g. 7-7-12) are best used on tomatoes and other fruiting crops. For instance, Tomorite, a well-known fertiliser for tomatoes, has a ratio of 24-27-48.

Understanding this and your plants' requirements can be useful but the world has become so fixated with fertilisers that we need a little perspective. Information about food and energy use on the Soil Association's website makes disturbing reading.

- It takes 1 tonne of oil and 108 tonnes of water to produce 1 tonne of artificial nitrogen and 7 tonnes of CO_2 greenhouse gases are produced in the process.[3]
- Nitrogen also produces nitrous oxide when it breaks down, a greenhouse gas over 300 times more powerful than carbon dioxide.
- Organic farming uses approximately 26 per cent less energy to produce the same amount of food as non-organic farming.

Plenty of reasons, therefore, to avoid artificial fertilisers and adopt a more organic approach. So obsessed has the world become with perfection and maximum yield that homeowners are guilty of using something like ten times more artificial fertiliser than commercial growers and the excess leaches into our streams and rivers.

Soil did pretty well before humans started messing about with it and gardeners are slowly coming round to the idea that ornamental plants don't need as much feeding as we are led to believe. It's reasonable to think that intensive use of land for food production will deplete the soil of nutrients to some degree, so improving the soil structure and aeration by adding organic matter should be your main objective as it helps nutrients already present in the soil to be more accessible to plants. A regular application each winter will, in most cases, be all that's necessary to keep your soil in good shape, with high potash liquid feeds made from comfrey leaves or dandelion roots to give fruiting crops a boost during their life cycle.

Compost

Good compost can make a big difference to the quality of your produce, and while it's easy enough to make, the difficulty is making enough of it. Three heaps at our plot don't provide anywhere near enough for our needs, and while imported compost runs the risk of being tainted with the chemical aminopyralid, which has ruined vegetables for many gardeners in recent years, we do get the

The beehive compost heap built with loosely-laid bricks.

---

[3] Just a sample of disturbing statistics from *An Inconvenient Truth about Food* published by the Soil Association.

occasional delivery of horse manure from a local stable.[4]

There are books and guides galore on the subject but the basic rule of thumb is that anything organic will rot down to compost given enough time. Most of it is common sense. Soft, sappy vegetation will break down more quickly than woody bulky twigs and branches. Balancing the right materials takes a little practice but essentially what you are aiming for is a mixture not too wet (too much grass-clippings and kitchen waste) and not too dry (too much woody material or shredded paper). Mix wet and dry materials and add them in layers so that the creatures and bacteria that go to work in a compost heap can move from one level to the next in unison and reduce the need for mixing.

Unless you are really organised and have a large enough heap to generate some serious heat, any seeds in the heap will germinate once you start spreading it, so avoid adding seedheads of annuals in the first place.

Books will also tell you not to add the roots of pernicious weeds to a heap. This is sensible advice although if they are first left somewhere near the heap to dry out and die, then there's no reason not to add the roots of bindweed, ground elder or couch grass. Even if they do turn out to be zombies and stage a comeback, the white roots of these weeds are easy to spot in the dark, friable compost when you come to use it and are easily removed. However, please don't even think of adding Japanese knotweed to a compost heap as it has powers of survival that defy earthly logic. If you see any evidence of it on an allotment, report it to the local authority.

Liquid manure

Liquid manure is an extremely useful tonic for plants and vegetables and a cost-saving substitute for expensive liquid fertilisers. It's easy to make too.

Russian comfrey (*Symphytum* × *uplandicum*) is the favourite ingredient as it holds more nutrients in its leaves than most plants, is quick to break down and is easy to propagate from root cuttings. Leaves and stems are put into a large container, covered with water and left for two or three weeks to decompose. The ensuing bilge stinks but is black gold for plants containing a good helping of nitrogen (N), phosphorus (P), potassium (K) and other minerals to boot.[5] Strain the liquid (put any bits on the compost heap) and dilute to approximately one-third fertiliser to two-thirds water before applying to plants. Don't get too het up about quantities and dilutions. As long as it looks like medium to weak tea you won't damage your plants in any way. Most people use it on tomatoes and other fruiting crops that benefit from a high potash feed but you can use it on anything; just be careful not to

TOP Comfrey leaves soaking in water.
BOTTOM Nettle leaves also make a good liquid manure.

---

[4] Aminopyralid is a herbicide used by farmers on grazing land. The hormone weedkiller is ingested by cattle, excreted and then finds its way to private gardens in composted manure sold by garden centres, etc. The effect on crops can be devastating, particularly for potatoes, tomatoes, legumes, carrots and lettuce.

[5] Taking the lid off a tub of fermenting comfrey leaves is like inspecting the blow-hole of a whale with halitosis and is therefore a useful deterrent if you find yourself cornered by a chatterbox.

A hessian sack, stuffed with leaves being put into a water butt to soak.

get it all over leaf vegetables that you are about to eat.

Other plants used for liquid manure are nettles and (for a higher potash feed) chopped up dandelion roots.[6] In fact all sappy green waste from lawn clippings to weeds are potential ingredients for liquid manure.

Green manure

Another way of overcoming the problems associated with sandy soil is to use green manure. Green manures are plants that help fertilise the soil when they are dug in and/or help stop nutrients from being washed away in winter as they grow. Used well they can reduce our dependency on imported compost. Often we grow them with other vegetables but we have to be careful about sowing times so they don't compete with vegetables in the early stage of their growth.

I was tuned into this by Iain Tolhurst, who runs a stockfree organic farm from a 500-year-old walled garden on the Hardwick Estate near Whitchurch-on-Thames, Oxfordshire.[7] It's a closed system, a method that uses no animal fertilisers – only green manures and home-made compost to feed the soil. It works better on a large scale where bands of green manure not only feed the soil but act as effective shelter belts for insects to create the ideal balance in biodiversity.

On an allotment the most effective way of using green manure might be to leave a bed fallow for a year and just grow nitrogen-fixing alfalfa or red clover to give the soil a rest. Mustard is also an interesting green manure as it has biofumigant properties (naturally occurring gases no less) in the leaves that can, by boosting the activity of beneficial soil microbes, suppress soil-borne diseases. For our green manure we mostly sow phacelia in late summer for its beautiful flowers. Crimson clover also has stunning flowers but the slugs on our plot are besotted with it so it never stands a chance. Fenugreek (*Trigonella foenum-graecum*) we try now and then as its leaves are a good substitute for spinach, but the most sensible green manures for us are Hungarian or winter-grazing rye and winter tares. These we sow in early autumn wherever there is bare soil from which nutrients might leach over the course of a wet winter. As the plants grow they help lock in nutrients and, when they are dug back into the soil in late winter/ early spring, they add a little organic matter to feed the soil. Leaving the plants to get too woody will not only make life difficult when it comes to digging but also take longer for the tough stems to break down in time for planting seeds.

A good garden centre should stock a reasonable range of green manures. Other varieties can be sourced online from companies such as Suffolk Herbs (www.suffolkherbs.com), The Organic Gardening Catalogue (www.organiccatalog. com) or Green Manure Seeds (www.greenmanure.co.uk).

Green manure being dug back into the soil before the stems become too woody.

[6] A tip from an article in 'Midnight brambling', the excellent blog by Lia Leendertz.

[7] Stockfree farms are those that have no grazing animals and no animal input to any part of the growing process.

List of green manures

Nitrogen-fixing green manures
- Crimson clover (*Trifolium incarnatum*), as a catch crop (a fast-growing crop between plantings of main crop) – sow July–early September
- Lucerne/alfalfa (*Medicago sativa*), for use as a ley crop – sow April–July
- Red clover (*Trifolium pratense*), for use as a ley crop – sow early September
- Trefoil (*Medicago lupulina*), for undersowing below taller crops – sow April–early September
- Vetch or winter tares (*Vicia sativa*), for undersowing below taller crops – sow April–early September

Green manures to reduce leaching
- Buckwheat (*Fagopyrum esculentum*) – sow April–early September
- Winter-grazing rye (*Secale cereale*) – sow September–November
- Mustard (*Sinapsis alba*) – sow March–September
- Phacelia (*Phacelia tanacetifolia*) – sow April–August

Modules

Most of our vegetables, whether they are hardy or not, start their life in modules or 9cm pots. Salad leaves, brassicas, beetroot, peas and beans are all molly-coddled until they reach a decent size to give them a fighting chance against the slugs. I wish this wasn't the case. Those who sow seeds directly into the soil and use slug pellets get far better results, especially when it comes to brassicas. The only seeds we sow direct

Beetroot is very happy growing in modules.

Potato foliage is particularly attractive to slugs as both a place to graze and reside. They are living in their dinner no less.

are radishes (which are quick to germinate), spring onions, parsnips and leeks. Leeks, a winter staple for us, get off to a much better start in open ground than in a pot. Most plants are happier in open soil as they are less likely to suffer from erratic watering and are able to draw minerals and trace elements that might be absent in manufactured potting composts. For our modules we use New Horizon peat-free compost, which suits most of our needs and doesn't dry out so quickly compared with other brands.

The period just after planting out the modules feels like a sort of limbo, a twilight zone where molly-coddled plants are at last on their own and at risk from all the things that share the allotment with us. It's an anxious time as very often a plant will sit, like a rabbit caught in the headlights, bewildered and perturbed at being placed in the big wide world. This is accentuated during a dry or cool spell when, far from the cosseted environment of the greenhouse, temperatures and humidity can fluctuate wildly. A heavy rainfall during a warm spell usually gets them going but this will also bring out slugs in their thousands, so night-time forays for us are a necessity if we are to stand any chance of keeping our plants alive. If you have the space, a cold frame can help plants acclimatise to an outdoor environment. Once plants are big enough to fend for themselves we can relax a little, even to the point of sowing successional seed direct into the now warm soil as, by this time, there is plenty for slugs to eat. They even eat weeds.

Maintaining a plot

For those who are trying to decide on whether to take on an allotment or not, this might be the most important section of the whole book. I've already pointed out that a large percentage of newcomers give up their allotments within two years. At least that's what the records say at the local council. In reality they probably give up a lot sooner, but the time it takes to ascertain whether someone is tending their plot or just making token gestures once or twice a year to keep the council off their back can take a while. This is frustrating for people on waiting lists and even more so when the allotment owner turns out to be living in another part of the country but has failed to give up their tenancy for whatever reason.

Romantic as they sound, allotments need regular attention to keep them productive. How much time? Well, if you're growing food to save money, whatever you do don't add up the time it takes to produce your own food and apply an hourly rate to it. It will only depress you. The National Society of Allotment and Leisure Gardeners (NSALG) estimates that, for a five rod plot (250 square metres), a gardener will spend just over 200 hours a year tending it. That sounds about right. We each spend at least one full day a week at the plot and often more during the busy period of sowing and growing between March and July.[8] This will be either a solid day over the weekend or a couple of hours here and there whenever we can spare the time. Oh, and by the way, when I say a day I don't mean office hours, I'm talking of at least twelve

---

[8] It's worth remembering that we have a larger than average plot. Officially we have 20 rods but in reality it amounts to about 15 rods of workable land.

Gardening at a distance from home can be testing, especially with our 'no-kill' policy. Growing plants in modules and pots gives them a useful head start and protecting crops while they are in the ground is essential if we are to ensure a measure of success.

Watering at an allotment can take up a huge amount of time during drought.

hours. A disciplined approach with a routine helps to make the work less onerous and I've found the best time to get quality work done is in the early morning. The benefits of having more energy, less distraction and higher mains pressure for more efficient watering outweigh the hassle of getting up at first light. You also get to see more wildlife and collect more slugs as they make the most of the morning dew, the only time they can get about in a drought.

How much can we grow?

People also ask, 'Just how much food can I expect to grow on a typical allotment?' As I've already said, we are not self-sufficient as that would require a much more organised approach but rarely do we have to buy seasonal vegetables and fruit and often have so much that we have to give it away. In other words, I haven't a clue. But I know a man who does: Phil Iddison. Phil's attention to order, tidiness and efficient use of space maximises his plot's potential and the plot looks all the better for it. There are no shortcuts when it comes to crop protection either and a large fruit cage bulges with berries on bushes that, in turn, offer support and protection for broad beans and brassicas.

In fact, if this was a book about *how* to grow vegetables I would have asked Phil to write it for me. His plot is the benchmark we all aspire to and clearly shows that organisation is the secret to successful vegetable growing. So organised is he that much of his work and everything he harvests is recorded on a spreadsheet. Exactly where he finds time to grow food, record the data *and* have a life outside the allotment is a mystery, but obviously being an engineer gives him a massive advantage over the likes of us mere mortals who can't remember what we've planted half the time.

His data suggests that from a 5-rod plot (125 square metres), assuming you have the organisational skills and discipline of an engineer, you might reasonably expect to produce a couple of helpings of fruit and veg per day for two people in all but the leanest months.

Distorted foliage of runner beans caused by the aminopyralid herbicide, inadvertently added to our plot through imported manure. It also affects potatoes, tomatoes, carrots and lettuce.

He's also worked out that he averages 13 hours a week on his ten-rod plot not including travelling. Quite a chunk for anyone in full-time employment. Don't forget that this is an average. The lion's share of the work, as much as 20 hours a week, takes place during the peak summer months. It's worth remembering, too, that Phil is someone who works efficiently.

As far as I'm aware Phil doesn't waste his time making sheds, pizza, onion bhajees, miniature snowmen, sculpture, breadboards or drawings of mutant roots. Neither is he 100 per cent organic. This is not a snipe. If he does use chemicals he uses them responsibly and sparingly. People choose their own paths in horticulture and, after a decade of trying to grow vegetables without deliberately killing anything, I'm on the verge of changing my ways.

Crop rotation

Varying the type of vegetables you grow in the same patch of ground is common practice for all vegetable growers, organic or not. It's a good practice as it reduces the risk of pests and diseases getting a foothold, the most serious perhaps being clubroot, a disease that affects brassicas and is extremely difficult to eradicate, especially on acidic soils.[9] Most growers adopt a four-year cycle but a six-year cycle is worth thinking about. This may sound extreme but it's based on the fact that each group of vegetables have differing needs in terms of fertility.

Cucurbits, especially pumpkins and squash, are voracious feeders. They can be planted on a recently composted bed and can even be planted directly into a compost heap. Carrots, on the other hand, are at the other end of the scale and will grow happily in sand. The rota set out on the next page shows six categories of vegetables and the rotation is based on the differing fertility needs. That doesn't mean to say that you shouldn't feed any other soil than that which will grow pumpkins. All soil benefits from organic matter being added, especially when potatoes and legumes (peas and beans) are being grown, but some vegetables like alliums (the onion family) and umbellifers (carrots, parsnips, etc.) can be sensitive if the compost hasn't had time to break down. Compost added to soil in late autumn will decompose sufficiently come the spring planting. Brassicas generally follow legumes as they will benefit not only from the previous season's composting but also from the nitrogen-fixing roots of beans and peas which are left in the ground. Another advantage of rotating crops in this way is that the larger leaves of earlier crops help restrict weed growth, so by the time the more sensitive alliums and umbellifers are planted, weeding should be less onerous a task.

Having said that, there are years when, either bad planning, lack of space or wilful recklessness will have us planting potatoes in the same place for two years in a row. It really isn't the end of the world. In fact, some people plant the same veg in the same spot year after year without any apparent problems, so it's unlikely that catastrophe will strike the minute there's a lapse in husbandry.

---

[9] The ideal pH for brassicas is approximately 7.2, so the addition of hydrated lime is common practice to make an acidic soil more alkaline. This will also reduce the likelihood of clubroot occurring.

Our crop rotation

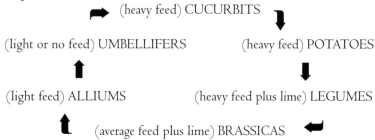

(heavy feed) CUCURBITS

(light or no feed) UMBELLIFERS

(heavy feed) POTATOES

(light feed) ALLIUMS

(heavy feed plus lime) LEGUMES

(average feed plus lime) BRASSICAS

Lunar planting

Whether you are a lunar planting convert or think that it's just a load of pagan nonsense repackaged for twenty-first-century New Ageists, the theory can, regardless of whether it works or not, be quite useful.

The idea is that the moon's gravitational pull affects fluid in plants and that, by timing your sowing, pruning and harvesting to coincide with the lunar calendar, you get a more successful crop. If you consider the effect of the moon on the earth's tides, water rising and falling, it's not as daft as it sounds. A waxing moon pulls while a waning moon pushes. Indeed, some believe it can even alter the fluids in our bodies affecting certain illnesses and behavioural patterns.[10]

A book by Nick Kollerstrom, *Gardening and Planting by the Moon*, makes the subject easier to digest and provides a calendar to tell you the best time to sow, prune, graft and harvest. Seed germination and transplanting is advised during a waxing moon when the moisture level in the soil is high, while pruning is better when the moon is waning and moisture is low (so the plant is less likely to bleed). The lunar cycle also uses the constellations of the zodiac: Earth (root crops), Water (leaf plants), Air (flowering plants) and Fire (fruit or seed plants), so that when, for example, the moon is in Taurus, Virgo or Capricorn (Earth signs) only tasks associated with earth-related veg (potatoes, carrots, parsnips, etc.) should be tackled. By planting, pruning and picking tomatoes when the moon is in Sagittarius (fire), the plant should grow with more vigour and health and harvested fruit will last longer.

Where it has helped us is in deciding what to do when we arrive at the plot on any given day, especially during March to July when it's difficult to decide what to concentrate on. A quick look at the chart at the plot tells us that it's a leaf day and all we need concentrate on is sowing or pricking out veg such as lettuce, chard, pak choi, cabbage, etc. The next time we visit might be a root day so beetroot, carrots and potatoes will get the attention they need. It focuses the mind and keeps us sane.

If you can only spend weekends gardening then this becomes a problem in which case my advice would be to let it go and plant when you can. On no account get worked up about it, as it will only cause hair in embarrassing places, goofy teeth and an undignified tendency to howl before supper. Believe me, I've been there.

---

[10] A nurse once told me that there was definitely more activity on the maternity wing at the hospital she worked whenever there was a full moon.

Biodynamics

Rudolf Steiner's studies into the influence of planetary rhythms on the growth of plants have taken organics and lunar gardening to another level by becoming increasingly popular with food growers around the world. I've always been fairly open-minded when it comes to gardening methods, willing to experiment and bend the rules a little, but I don't think I'm quite ready for biodynamics. Fermented vegetable, animal and mineral concoctions ranging from cow horns filled with manure or crushed quartz to animal bladders stuffed with herbs buried in compost heaps or stirred into a liquid preparation verge on witchcraft. Yet proponents of this science-cum-spiritual way of gardening swear by its effectiveness. Even some of my best friends are biodynamic. The vegetables I've seen for sale at Fern Verrow's stand at Borough Market are about as good as it gets in food production, so the proof is in the produce. Part of me is curious to explore these methods, so what it probably boils down to is that I haven't the patience for stirring. I'm willing to be converted but just need a bit more time.

Slug tips

While slugs and snails always seem to be at the top of the gardener's hate list, we've always held a quiet respect for their ways ever since finding a circle of 20 snails on our drive after a sudden downpour. It was a perfect circle, 60cm in diameter, with each snail either facing inward or slightly towards its neighbour, occasionally touching with antennae. You'll have to take my word for this, as there is no photographic evidence. The spectacle has given credence to the idea that they are more intelligent than most people give them credit for.

Slugs and snails operate most efficiently in damp conditions. They are much less active during dry weather but humid microclimates beneath plants, near building structures or among debris can be enough for them to make quick forays to find food nearby. With a little observation you'll get to know these areas and pay special attention to vegetables planted nearby, and of course make finding and removing them much easier for yourself. If you are particularly fastidious with no obvious habitat for slugs, remember that they can hide beneath the soil, so a small pile of bricks, logs or broken paving slabs placed somewhere convenient will help you target them quickly and leave you more time for other tasks.

Understanding the habits and knowing the habitats of slugs and snails will help you deal with them more effectively.

If you don't use slug pellets then you must keep a sharp eye on the weather when it comes to sowing seeds direct into open ground. As long as the seed is fresh, carrots and parsnips are not difficult to germinate but are quickly grazed by slugs, often before they've set their cotyledon leaves (first pair). They'll take a little more time to germinate than, say, lettuce (a couple of weeks), after which a window of dry weather is your best chance to establish them.

Watering plants in the evening may be efficient in terms of reducing evaporation, but if you are unwilling to do midnight forays then it's best to water during the day so that, come evening, the soil surface is dry enough to make life difficult for slugs and snails.

CHAPTER FOUR

Creativity

As a canvas for creativity, the allotment can provide endless opportunities. Christine, who studied textiles at Camberwell School of Art, is a printmaker and often draws inspiration from the allotment for her work. In an ideal world she would settle down to while away many creative hours with a sketchbook, but the reality is that there is usually far too much to do to immerse ourselves in anything creative during the summer months. Winter projects such as building a new shed or, more recently, a bread/pizza oven are absorbing, and quite often I find myself hoping that winter lingers long enough for us to indulge in these little divergences before the mad rush of spring sets us off at a new pace.

You don't need to be a designer to express yourself on an allotment.

Inevitably, caught up in the excitement of taking on a plot for the first time, mistakes were made in our first year in terms of practicalities. Circular raised beds made from ribbed plastic pipe left over from a show garden turned out to be completely impractical in terms of space and provided the perfect environment for slugs to hole up in during the day. I think it's called 'trying to be too clever'.

Of course, you don't need to be a designer to express yourself on an allotment. The very ramshackle nature of recycling, improvising and modifying means the plot is a natural canvas and inspiration for creativity. Decay in all its forms is more acceptable on an allotment than in an ornamental garden or public landscape. Rotting wood, rusting metal, moss, lichen and fungi are not just

the natural ingredients, they are the stars of the show. Nor are there any restrictions on materials at an allotment. Plastic, glass, toys, household objects and all sorts of rubbish have their own peculiar charm with the power to become a vignette of the life and character of the plot-holder. It's this that makes them so appealing. No judges, no press, no pressure to adhere to convention mean that, aside from neglecting it completely and risking a letter from the council, from a designer's perspective it's a bit like (ahem) vegging-out. Even when members of the Garden Museum came to visit one summer, there were no anxious moments rushing around, trying to make things presentable. Everything is as it is according to the amount of time you've had to spend on it that week.

Sheds

It may sound sad, but I don't think I could survive at the plot without a shed. The fact that I am currently building my fourth is, even in my book, a little excessive but there's a philanthropic logic behind it. With allotments being in such demand, our local council have taken to dividing up any 10-rod plots that become vacant, which is obviously a perfectly reasonable thing to do. With all the work we have put in over the years (especially when allotments weren't quite so in demand), I am loath to give up our plot without a fight, but when we do part company and the council come to carve up the rods, each plot will have its own shed and one will have a shed *and* a greenhouse.

Sheddism is traditionally a bloke thing but I think that's only because allotments have been their sole domain for so long. They offer boundless opportunities for creativity although, being built mostly from reclaimed timber, they usually evolve from whatever is available at the time. If I had control of the allotments I would ban prefabricated sheds and urge people to make their own in the name of local distinctiveness and individuality. Even those who are unable to build their own for whatever reason should coerce a friend to help them create something that adds a bit more personality to the place than that shown by orange, larch-lap boxes of mediocrity.

Building a shed is cathartic and best done over the winter so that you are not continuously battling with your conscience about other things you should be doing. For me, winter at the allotment is as enjoyable as the summer, if not more so. Being less busy, there is more time to feel at one with the place and catch up with tasks that are impossible even to consider when things are growing.

Each of our sheds has a green roof. They were originally planted with grasses and houseleeks but we eventually chose the more drought tolerant stonecrop (*Sedum acre*) which only needs watering after a month of drought. If there were more time I'm sure the sheds could be improved but they add a little character and will, I hope, provide useful storage for whoever inherits the plot when we leave.

The Wonky Shed, built during our first year at the plot, was not only a useful distraction from the fact that we hadn't a clue when it came to growing food, but its daft shape set the tone for future activities. It certainly added a lighter note to the place, but the fact that it was placed at 45 degrees led to an awkward, shady space behind it that was impractical and difficult to resolve. It eventually became a small ditch-like pond with a small bridge that teeters just on the acceptable side of tweeness but is a useful refuge for amphibians, ducks and small children. All we had succeeded in doing was to announce to other members of Bushy Park Allotment Association that here were newcomers with absolutely no idea how to go about growing vegetables and who

Building a shed is a cathartic experience. I would urge anyone taking on an allotment to resist any temptation to buy a prefabricated structure and make something that will add a touch of individuality to their plot.

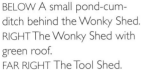

BELOW A small pond-cum-ditch behind the Wonky Shed.
RIGHT The Wonky Shed with green roof.
FAR RIGHT The Tool Shed.

would probably be gone by Christmas. It used to store all our tools but now houses all the things that we thought might be useful for the allotment (drawers, chairs, scraps of wood, metal, etc.) that we can't bring ourselves to throw away, and it's consequently stuffed to a point where opening the door involves evacuating at least two neighbouring plots so people don't get injured from the inevitable fall-out. A rabbit burrow under this shed makes good use of a secret chamber originally made to store valuables but abandoned when we realised that, aside from the dog, we didn't really having anything of value to store in it.

The Wonky Shed was absolutely the reason why we gave it another year but, of the four, this is the one that really ought to come down.

The Tool Shed was built on our second plot during a tedious bout of theft. Tools were being nicked during the night on a regular basis and so leaving anything of worth overnight became a serious risk. A shed without windows seemed to be the obvious solution and again I used as much reclaimed lumber as possible, much of it large and heavy, including a single slab of elm for the door. Complete with loft space for nesting birds, it looks a bit like a gun tower and makes a fine backdrop for an espaliered Conference pear.

A few weeks after I'd finished building the tool shed, I arrived at the plot to find that many of the neighbouring sheds had been upended and all the contents removed from underneath. Ours, the sole witness to the carnage, stood untouched like a brooding sentinel. So far so good.

The Potting Shed is bigger than what might be considered allowable on an allotment, but it was built on the footprint of an old dilapidated structure that we found on clearing the two plots behind us, so I figured it was okay. A sink filled with

The Potting Shed doubles as a makeshift kitchen and consequently exists in a perpetual state of upheaval.

compost and some shelving afford us the luxury of potting up in comfort while standing. A small thing, perhaps, but one that gives a disproportionate amount of satisfaction. Due to its location at the back of the plot where we tend to gather and eat, it has taken over from the Wonky Shed as the hub and doubles as a makeshift kitchen. The door to this shed was a souvenir from the BBC programme, *Small Town Gardens*, and it too sports a green roof, though this struggles in the shade. Lately we have made tumbleweed-like balls of muehlenbeckia prunings from our garden at home and placed them on the roof to detract from the slightly slapdash construction and offer birds more habitat in which to nest.

The Fourth Shed currently has no name and lies on the other side of the stream behind the greenhouse. Some might think this excessive but when we eventually give up the plot the council will almost certainly divide it up into four so each plot will be ready to go with its own custom-built shed. Garden designer, Tony Smith, has persuaded me to think about decorating it with artificial grass and has given me the moniker, 'Foursheds'.

Compost heaps

'Beehive' compost heaps built using reclaimed bricks made an attractive feature at the plot before I used all the bricks to make the base for the earth oven. I'd first seen them in a friend's garden where several large kiln-like forms had been constructed at the bottom of his garden with their contents each at a different stage of decomposition. They had straight sides and stood 1.2m high and 1.8m in diameter; some held leaf-mould, others regular garden waste and grass clippings. On removing a section

Filled with fresh manure and a cap of topsoil, a beehive compost heap can make a useful raised bed for cucurbits.

of bricks I was astonished to find a quality of compost I had never seen before. Rich and dark like the best Dundee cake you could ever imagine, it really did look edible.

With the bricks laid loose, without mortar, these bins are easy to construct if you have a reasonably good eye for shape and form. The art is in preparing a level base and then laying the bricks carefully, using a spirit level if you want straight sides or stepping each successive course slightly inward if you want something like the classic beehive shape. This not only makes it look more interesting but also adds extra strength to the structure, making it less likely to collapse.

Bean supports

Large wigwams of hazel sticks tied at the top with a ball of chain have become our signature structure. These are simple but striking, adding some much needed verticality to the plot while animating it, bringing it to eerie life on misty mornings when the arachnid forms loom mysteriously from autumnal mists.

When I had a van we would collect our hazel sticks from Laurence Crow, a forester we have known for some years in Capel, Surrey. A trip to his bluebell woods in early summer to pick them up became something of a tradition. Since the van bit the dust we have been fortunate to have the topiary expert, James Crebbin-Bailey, supply us with prunings from his own garden.

These supports are easy to erect and striking to look at even without runner beans. A minimum of three poles per leg of each tripod are used to ensure stability and to stop the structure buckling under the weight of not only the chain ball but the climbing beans themselves. Supple when new, the poles lend themselves to being shaped and bent, and will last a season before they become brittle and a danger to anyone working nearby in a gale.

Mutant roots

A series of drawings known as 'Mutant Roots' were inspired by the notion that growing root vegetables is a bit like archaeology in that the unearthed roots have never been seen before. Naturally enough it led me to imagine what sort of vegetables, as yet undiscovered, might lie beneath our feet. Ricky Gervais's *Flanimals* (which annoyingly came out as I'd finished the first set) put me off progressing the idea and the drawings have spent most of their life in a drawer.

Sculpture

Having studied art at college, worked for a fine art publishing company and enjoyed fruitful collaborations with Johnny Woodford and Serge and Agnes Bottagisio-Decoux, sculpture in gardens has always interested me and the allotment has always seemed a natural place for creative expression.

ABOVE Simple wigwam structures give a useful vertical accent to a vegetable plot for beans and cucurbits to scramble over. Hazel sticks tied with chain have become a regular feature on our plot.
BELOW Finding the time to make sculpture at the allotment is rare but spontaneous use of found objects can be enough to curb any sense of frustration.

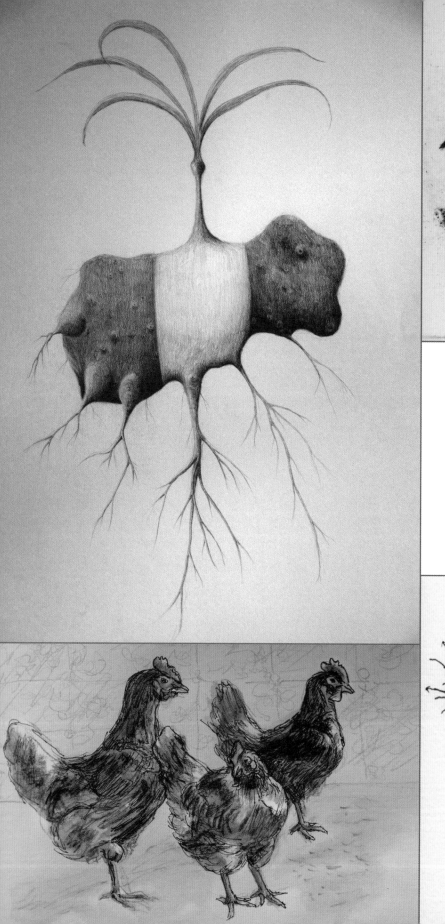

As a printmaker, Christine often draws inspiration from the natural world, crows and jackdaws being a recurrent theme. Naturally, when there is time, the plot is a useful muse for her. My own plot-inspired pencil doodles, fanciful notions of what might lie beneath, manifested themselves into a series of drawings known as 'Mutant Roots'.

The idea has been to pepper the plot with a mixture of (found) *objets d'art* and spontaneous works made from old bits of timber, stone and metal, something akin to the spirit of Derek Jarman's garden at Dungeness. The reality is that there is rarely the time to indulge in such fantasies but occasionally we find a moment to vent a little creative expression.

Scarecrows

Compared with pigeons and squirrels, crows are the least of our concerns, but scarecrows have obvious potential for creativity and they do pop up on other plots from time to time. I once made a temporary one in a Brentford FC football shirt for a newspaper article, but the scarecrows I really want to make are quite dark in spirit and may frighten small children. They will have to stay on the back burner for now.

Snowmen

Being caught at the plot making miniature snowmen was much less embarrassing than being caught taking pictures of Beth Chatto's tights. I should point out here that Mrs Chatto wasn't wearing the said tights at the time. They were being used to catch the seed of *Euphorbia myrsinites*. It was only when I got close up to them with my macro lens that I realised they weren't some sort of unusual seedhead. The snowmen have since become something of a tradition.

Miniature snowmen have become something of a custom at our plot. Each one takes just a few seconds to make.

11th January 2007

Arrived at the plot early this morning to dig leeks and feed birds before going to the office when it started snowing. Hasn't snowed here for years so stayed to see what it would do. Small flakes quickly turned fat and lumpy covering the plot quickly. Made a brew then watched and listened as the plot is cloaked and silenced. Forms now accentuated including seed put out for birds which morph into abstract figures. Three miniature snowmen no less. Snow perfect for making small shapes and our table is soon covered with geeky bird-like figures not unlike ephemeral love-children of some Goldsworthy–Gormley collaboration. Natasha arrives with her children and looks slightly awkward as if she's caught me doing something completely inappropriate for a man of my age. Am too excited to care. Spontaneity hugely refreshing and I arrive at the office four hours late relieved that I am self-employed.

Winter affords us the time to catch up on chores that there just isn't time for during the main growing season. It also allows us to dream a little.

CHAPTER FIVE

Vegetables and herbs

Asparagus is a permanent crop so a useful one to grow if you want to simplify things.

The following list is not exhaustive. It is a note of the vegetables and herbs we grow or have at least flirted with in some way. Taste is very personal so don't take the varieties we've tried as gospel. Cross refer to other books and, of course, fellow plot-holders, especially those who have had plots for some years. I've tried to give an idea of quantities by noting the number of plants we grow and whether we have succeeded in growing just enough (for two people), too much or found ourselves left wanting.

It's very embarrassing to have to admit that, over the course of ten years, our annual crop of asparagus is still so pathetic that we have to buy it in. The worst thing about having to buy vegetables when your crops fail is that most of them are wrapped in plastic. It makes no sense.

Asparagus (*Asparagus officinalis*)

One vegetable that has eluded us for much of our time is asparagus, largely because we didn't prepare the ground sufficiently before planting. Couch grass and bindweed have defeated us and the few shoots that do appear are thinner than a flea beetle's antenna. The annoying thing is that while our soil is a bit lean for the majority of crops we grow, it's actually perfect for asparagus. Bleating about weeds is therefore about as lame as it gets.

Like rhubarb and artichoke, asparagus is a permanent crop so a useful one to grow if you want to simplify things. Seed will take three years before you can first harvest. Buying crowns will save you a year and then you must religiously keep the bed weed free and well fertilised. Once established you will not only have one of the best tasting vegetables around but also one of the most expensive.

Raised beds are, in theory, easier to weed but rotting timber is the perfect habitat for slugs and snails to lay their eggs in, so keep it well maintained. I'm hoping that this book may serve as a catalyst for knocking my own bed into shape so that one day I'll experience a level of smugness hitherto unknown on our plot.

By the way, overcooking asparagus (five minutes is all it needs) is the most serious foodie crime on the planet.

Sow: February under cover.

Plant out: May–June for seedlings, March–April for crowns.

Spacing: Approx. 60cm apart in rows 80cm apart.

Harvest: Late April–June (three years after planting seed, two years after planting crowns).

Quantity: You can't grow enough of this delicacy as you will be very popular if you have a glut. Our six crowns, once they get going, should be enough to keep us happy.

Note: Don't overharvest young crops.
Varieties: 'Connover's Colossal'; 'Mary Washington'; 'Millennium' (F1).

Aubergine *(Solanum melongena)*

We've grown aubergine but not in sufficient quantity to stop us lying prostrate and worshipping every one that reaches the plate. They're easy enough to get started in modules, accommodating when it comes to transplanting and always obliging with their delightful flowers, a reason in itself for growing them. I think where it all goes pear-shaped is in our greenhouse management. They like it hot but extremes can give them the jitters, and I don't think we mist them enough or jiggle the flowers to help with the pollinating … oh and we always forget to stake them, so if the slugs don't get the fruit that touches the ground the woodlice will. It's not that we're not used to holes in veg, they're an organic seal of approval, but there's something unholy about the tainted purity that is a nibbled aubergine. It's really very disappointing.

Sow: January–March under cover.
Plant out: May–June.
Spacing: 60cm apart.
Harvest: August–October.
Quantity: In a good year six plants should give us just enough.
Note: Best grown indoors but can be grown outside in a warm sheltered spot.
Varieties: 'Black Beauty'; 'De Barbentane'; 'Diamond'.

Basil *(Ocimum basilicum)*

Despite its Mediterranean connotations, basil originates in India and Iran. There are many varieties and it's worth experimenting but the common Sweet Basil is hard to beat. Pesto made using fresh basil leaves that you've grown yourself and made within minutes of harvesting makes jars of ready-made pesto quite synthetic by comparison. A sprinkling of seed into 3-litre pots every couple of weeks and you'll have basil to hand all through summer. That makes it sound easy and really it is except for two things: (a) they need warmth to grow well and (b) they should only be watered in the morning to stop them damping off or sulking.

Sow: Late April–May onwards.
Plant out: Late June.
Spacing: 20cm in rows 30cm apart.
Harvest: July–October.
Quantity: We sow two 3-litre pots every three weeks from May to July and have just enough.
Note: Harden off seedlings before planting outside in a warm spot. Bring basil growing in pots indoors at the end of September to prolong the growing period.
Varieties: 'Lemon Basil'; 'Purple Basil'; 'Sweet Basil'.

Beetroot *(Beta vulgaris)*

Good old beetroot. It's one of the most accommodating and reliable crops we grow and a must for anyone starting a veg plot. It's also one of those vegetables that really

Aubergine, as you can see, is revered as much by slugs as by us. Very annoying!

Basil

does taste better when you grow it yourself and harvest it young. (A teacher at my old school often recounted the fact that they used to dye the house rugby team's shirts with beetroot. Our house colour was red but a T-shirt I tried dying with beetroot came out pink so I can only imagine how that particular first XV must have felt as they ran out onto the pitch.)

We grow lots of beetroot for the young leaves which can be used in salad, and smaller beets taken to help thin a row are as sweet as they come, beautiful baked with garlic and thyme and a little balsamic vinegar.

Anyone indifferent to beetroot should reserve judgement for the small roots, which are much sweeter than its earthy tasting reputation. They are easy to grow and attractive, even in a flower border. If you've never been a fan of beetroot but are now tempted, don't panic when you go to flush the loo the morning after you've gorged on your first plateful.

Sow: March–June under cover, April–July direct.

Plant out: May–July.

Spacing: 10cm apart in rows 20cm apart.

Harvest: July–October.

Quantity: Two 3m rows in spring and another two in July are more than enough and allow us to give some away.

Note: Wider spacings will allow them to grow bigger but the smaller ones are sweeter.

Varieties: 'Bolthardy'; 'Cylindra'; 'Sanguina'.

Beetroot is one of the most reliable crops. The leaves can be eaten as a spinach substitute.

Bottle gourd or Louka (Nepal) or Bau (Vietnam)
(*Lagenaria vulgaris*)

Sow: March–May under cover, in 9cm pots.
Spacing: 1m apart.
Harvest: September–October.
Quantity: One!! (See diary note.)
Note: The flesh of this gourd is more tender picked young when you can still pierce the skin with your fingernail. Great in stir-fries as it holds its texture.

Broad bean (*Vicia fabia*)

I hated these as a kid. In fact parents who feed large and overcooked broad beans to their children should be reported to the social services for cruelty to children. Picking pods while they are still young and tender, however, will reveal beans that have a more delicate, sweeter taste and give you an annual treat that even children will really look forward to.

November sowings of 'Aquadulce Claudia' get a good head start the following spring so that you can harvest by May. Leaves will also have toughened up enough to make them slightly less vulnerable to slugs.

Nip out the top buds when the first pods start to swell (about three or four trusses of flowers) as this will help direct energy to the developing pods. It also helps to control blackfly as they like these tender leaves. Don't waste these tender tops as they are a delicious steamed and eaten with a little butter drizzled over them.

Sow: November and February–May direct, 5cm deep.
Spacing: 20cm apart in rows 60cm apart.
Harvest: May–October.

Quantity: Two rows of 3m are OK but a later sowing of another two rows will extend the season.
Note: If blackfly persist after pinching out the tops, make a slurry of mud and water and rub some of it over the tips to make life difficult for them.
Varieties: 'Aquadulce Claudia'; 'Crimson Flowered' (for its crimson flowers obviously); 'Imperial Green Longpod'; 'The Sutton' (dwarf variety).

6ᵗʰ August 2010

The whole mood inside the greenhouse has changed. With tomatoes doing their usual sulk at our inability to give them everything they need, a mixture of vines give the illusion that we are actually quite good at growing things. The Black Hamburg (a cutting from the vine at Hampton Court), which has spent the last three seasons not knowing where it stands in the world, has at last been invited in through a broken pane of glass on the east side and now runs along the apex of the roof all the way to the door at the west. Adding a verdant display of foliage are cucumbers and a Nepali cucurbit called Louka, which, despite growing a foot a day, flowering and poking its head through the roof, still hasn't produced anything suitably long and dangly. Dhundi gave us the seed so I call him to find out what to expect. He can't remember what the fruit looks like but apparently the vine grows to 40 foot. Now he tells us! I decide to pollinate the flowers myself and after a few minutes looking for the paintbrush find that the vine has coiled round and secreted it to the ceiling of the greenhouse, the craftiest act of thieving I have seen at the plot to date.

ABOVE Bottle gourd.
LEFT Crimson flowers of the rather appropriately named 'Crimson Flowered' broad bean variety.

Brussels sprouts

Brussels sprout (*Brassica oleracea* var. *gemmifera*)

Our sprout harvest was so bad one season it felt as though the whole year had been ruined largely because the vegetables we can pick fresh on Christmas morning have become our yardstick for success. Sprouts are not difficult to grow but, like all brassicas, need a soil pH of 6.5–7. Too acid and you risk the dreaded clubroot. Soil testing kits are widely available and easy to use. Dressing with lime will raise the pH. Approximately 1kg of lime per square metre will raise pH from 5.5 to 6.5.

Sprouts take some time and will be ripped to shreds by pigeons if not suitably protected. They prefer a more fertile and heavier soil than ours so we plant them after beans, whose nitrogen-fixing roots have been left in the ground, and make sure that the ground is firm for their roots to get a good foothold. Compact soil will help stop the sprouts from 'blowing'. Earthing-up around the stems and consolidating the soil is good practice in sandy soils.

Sow: February–April.

Plant out: April–May.

Spacing: Approx. 60cm apart.

Harvest: August–March.

Quantity: Six plants will give us sprouts for around ten meals. We're sparing to begin with so that we have enough to share for Christmas Day, after which they disappear very quickly. We could easily use more but never seem to have enough space.

Note: We find that the later cropping varieties are better. Who wants to eat sprouts in summer anyway?

Varieties: 'Bedford Fillbasket'; 'Igor' (F1); 'Sanda'; 'Seven Hills'.

Cabbage (*Brassica oleracea* var. *capitata*)

I can't say cabbages have been top of my wish list over the years, but there's something wholesome about growing them yourself and watching them bulge out to produce a fine array of shapes and colours to keep you going through the leaner months of

Cabbage

winter and early spring. Savoy-types are our favourites. Needless to say, slugs like them too. I always think that if a vegetable has been nibbled a bit then it's proof that it's organic, and each of our cabbages can still provide several meals no matter how bad it looks from the outside. However, I must admit that there are times when the number of slugs killed just by slicing a cabbage in half can really put you off your tea.

Sow: In August for spring cabbage and April–June for summer to winter harvests.

Plant out: When four or five true leaves have developed.

Spacing: 30–45cm each way depending on variety.

Harvest: Spring cabbage in April and winter crops between October and late February.

Quantity: Two rows of 3m of winter and spring cabbage are plenty for us.

Note: Don't let the seedlings dry out as this will check their growth.

Varieties: 'January King' (winter); 'Precoce de Louviers' (spring); 'Red Drumhead' (summer).

Cardoon (*Cynara cardunculus*)

They may look similar but globe artichokes and cardoons are quite different when it comes down to what each vegetable yields in the kitchen. Aesthetically, both are about as eye-catching as you can get and can make a valuable contribution to an ornamental garden.

If I'm honest I like the plant more for its exotic appearance than for its taste but that might have something to do with my culinary skills. Mark Diacono, at Otter Farm, has sworn to put that to rights one day.

Sow: March–April under cover.

Plant out: Late May.

Spacing: Approx. 80cm–1m apart.

Harvest: September–November.

Quantity: One plant is enough.

Note: Cook soon after harvesting as the stems lose their rigidity after being cut.

Varieties: 'Gigante di Romagna' (according to Mark Diacono).

Cardoon

Carrot (*Daucus carota*)

In the early years we thought that the carrots weren't germinating but it was just that they were being grazed at the cotyledon stage. Perseverance and a little luck with the weather is the only chance we have of growing them. A drought in spring may not be perfect for growing vegetables, but slugs don't travel when it's dry and that's something we have to exploit. Watering in the morning ensures that come nightfall the soil's surface is dry again, making it difficult for slugs to move about. Not ideal from a water-wise point of view but it's the only chance we have of getting carrots on the plate.

Carrot fly is another problem. Earlier (March/April) sowings need fleece protection but later (May/June) sowings germinate more quickly and are less likely to suffer from the fly.

Sow: Mid-March–June.

Plant out or thin: April–mid-July.

Spacing: Thin to 5cm between plants; wider if you want larger roots.

Harvest: June–November.

Quantity: We plant a row of 3m or resow gaps where they have been grazed by slugs every few weeks. In a good year, when they are left untouched, four rows of 3m will keep us going until the New Year.

Note: Carrots are best sown direct but you can sow in modules as long as you plant them out before they get too big so that their main tap-root can continue to grow freely.

Varieties: 'Amsterdam Forcing'; 'Autumn King'; 'Lisse de Meaux'; 'Nantes'.

Carrots

Celeriac (*Apium graveolens* var. *rapaceum*)

We've grown them before so it is possible, but they need more water and extra care than we give them, and for some unknown reason we plant them later than we should so they invariably look runtish compared with Ted's monsters. However, thanks to Ted's continuous generosity, we never go without.

Celeriac

Chard

Chilli

Chives

Sow: February–March under cover.
Plant out: May–June.
Spacing: 30–40cm apart.
Harvest: September–March.
Quantity: Two 3m rows are plenty.
Note: Ted is always on the case not to waste the stalks of this mighty vegetable, which can add character to a soup.
Varieties: 'Del Veneto'; 'Printz'.

Chard *(Beta vulgaris* subsp. *cicla* var. *flavescens)*

Chard is closely related to perpetual spinach (*Beta vulgaris* subsp. *cicla* var. *cicla*). Both will provide leaves all year round, are relatively easy to maintain and, with a range of colours to choose from, are often used just to add colour to a veg patch or even an ornamental border. Chard lacks the refinement and subtle texture of true spinach (*Spinacia oleracea*) but chard and perpetual spinach are easier to grow, largely because the leaves are thicker and therefore less susceptible to grazing by slugs.

Sow: March–April under cover, May–August direct.
Plant out: April–May.
Spacing: 40cm.
Harvest: Year round.
Quantity: Six plants keep us going once established.
Note: The central stem cooks more slowly than the leaf and is best cut out and cooked separately.
Varieties: 'Argentata'; 'Bright Lights'; 'Golden Chard'; 'Ruby Chard'; 'Sibilla'.

Chilli *(Capsicum annuum)*

Reckless overuse of these fiery-hot peppers can ruin a meal for those with a sensitive palate but just a dash of heat can elevate flavours to a different level. More and more people are discovering the magic of chillies and becoming more adventurous with their cooking. Easy to grow, these plants warrant a place in any garden.

Sow: February–April under cover.
Plant out: June.
Spacing: 30–40cm apart.
Harvest: August–October.
Quantity: Three plants are enough for us but invariably we grow more and give them away.
Note: Chillies need warmth to get them started. Sow them earlier rather than later to give them a chance to mature.
Varieties: 'Anaheim' (slightly hot); 'Biala Shipka' (very hot); 'Habanero' varieties (call the fire brigade).

Chive *(Allium schoenoprasum)*

Pretty flowers add to the charm of this perennial kitchen herb. It's dead easy to grow so no garden should be without it.

Sow: March.

Plant out: May.

Spacing: Plant approx. 20cm apart in rows or just grow them where there is space.

Harvest: Regularly once mature to encourage new leaves.

Quantity: Four or five clumps or pots allow us a regular harvest.

Note: Established clumps can be divided easily in spring. Ask a friend to give you some.

TOP Herbs like chop suey greens are rarely available in the shops.
MIDDLE Others, like coriander, are ridiculously over-priced and over-packaged so it's worth growing your own if you can.
BOTTOM Courgette.

Chop suey greens or Shungiku (*Chrysanthemum coronarium* var. *spatiosum*)

A flavoursome chrysanthemum, the young leaves of which are good for stir-fry, salad, sag or soup. The flowers are a beautiful bonus and provide seed to keep you going forever.

Sow: Early spring to autumn direct for a succession of leaves.

Plant out: June onwards.

Spacing: Sow generously and thin as required.

Harvest: Before flowers develop unless you are making 'Kikumi', a Japanese pickle made from the flower petals.

Quantity: One 3m row is more than enough for us.

Note: Sow in autumn under glass for a winter crop.

Coriander (*Coriandrum sativum*)

At around a pound for a small sprig of coriander in supermarkets, it's definitely a herb worth growing if you can. My Anglo-Indian roots mean that I rely heavily on this herb throughout the year for curries and sauces, so ideally I should be harvesting armfuls of it come summer. I might as well try to grow gold. Notorious for setting seed when it gets stressed or has too much sun, there only needs to be a slight change in our routine or a delay in watering for it to get the hump. If I grew it at home I would sow seed directly into the soil in part shade where it would stand a much better chance of doing well. It's not a disaster if your crop runs to seed as the seed can also be used in the kitchen.

Quantity: If we could get it to grow properly, a couple of rows sown every few weeks would be very welcome as we use a lot of it.

Sow: April–May direct or in deep containers.

Spacing: 1cm deep and 4cm apart in drills 15cm apart. Thin to 20cm apart.

Harvest: Before they flower, if it's the leaves you want to use.

Note: Resow every three weeks.

Varieties: 'Confetti'; 'Santos'.

Courgette (*Cucurbita pepo*)

This is another good vegetable to start with, especially if your vegetable garden is quite large, as the broad leaf cover helps to smother and suppress weeds. Aside from keeping the slugs at bay in the early stages, courgettes require little by way of maintenance. Plant early and late to extend your harvest and to stop you from getting

The 'Miniature White' cucumber actually goes yellow as it matures and is best eaten young.

a glut which might put you off them altogether. Pick when young unless you want marrows. We prefer the yellow varieties, which are sweeter.

Sow: April–June under cover.
Plant out: May–July.
Spacing: Approx. 60cm apart.
Harvest: July–October.
Quanity: Two plants give us enough for ourselves and some to share.
Note: Keep an eye on the weather when planting out as a late frost will set them back or kill them.
Varieties: 'Black Milan'; 'Jemmer' (FI, yellow); 'Parador' (FI, yellow).

Cucumber (*Cucumis sativus*)

The growth rate of cucumbers is phenomenal. They take a while to get going, but once established you won't be able to pick and eat them quickly enough. They are very useful for small gardens and balconies, where they can be trained up plant supports, and are equally happy finding their own way through a herbaceous border. Apart from keeping them watered they are quite undemanding.

Sow: April–May under cover.
Plant out: June.
Spacing: 60cm.
Harvest: July–October.
Quantity: Three plants are sufficient.
Note: We plant them randomly wherever there is space for them to scramble. Pick and eat them young when they are at their crunchy best.
Varieties: 'Crystal Lemon'; 'Miniature White'; 'Mirella'; 'Wautoma'.

While we have been successful with Florence fennel, my pictures have been less so. Over to Christine.

Florence fennel (*Foeniculum vulgare* var. *azoricum*)

The secret to growing this bulbous fennel without it bolting is to sow it later than usual and hope that an Indian summer will fatten the bulbs sufficiently before the first frosts. Late May sowings should give you a reasonable return by late September, assuming regular watering and reasonable fertility. Braised slowly to release their sugary potential, these bulbs are a real treat and a fine transitional vegetable from summer salads to winter soups.

Sow: April–July direct.
Spacing: 25cm apart.
Harvest: June–November.
Quantity: Two 3m rows are enough for us.
Note: 'Finale' is less likely to bolt.
Varieties: 'Colossal'; 'Finale'; 'Romanesco'.

Geoff Noakes (on the right) is well known for his prize-winning vegetables and in particular his incredible collection of cucurbits. Known affectionately as 'The Gourdfather', I once had the pleasure of meeting him at his allotment in Coldean, near Brighton, and seeing this fabulously colourful array of squash, pumpkins and gourds looking like crash-landed satellites. With over 100 varieties, Geoff is occasionally asked to supply food and decoration for the tables at Petersham Nurseries.

French bean (*Phaseolus vulgaris*)

Less stringy than runner beans, French beans have become a favourite with us, particularly as they are more difficult to come by in the shops. They are still liable to get 'beany' very quickly and should be eaten young. Fresh off the vine, they serve as a useful breakfast on early morning sessions. If you can't snap the ends off when preparing, then they're not good enough for the kitchen.

Again, outwitting slugs is the only real problem with growing beans. They have the advantage of looking attractive and can easily be incorporated into a small garden where space is tight. Runner beans need more watering and can get stringy so we mostly grow French climbing beans these days.

Sow: March–May under cover, May–July direct.

Plant out: From May when no danger of frost.

Spacing: 20cm apart as a general rule of thumb, whether in a line or around a wigwam structure.

Harvest: July–October.

Quantity: Six plants keep us happy. We occasionally plant a late batch to extend the season. If you are short there is always someone who has a glut and is pleased to give you some.

Note: Sow a late batch at the end of July to have beans well into October.

Varieties: 'Cherokee Trail of Tears'; 'Cosse de Violet'; 'Purple Teepee'.

French beans

Garlic (*Allium sativum*)

As a symbol of growth and a beacon of hope clearly showing that there is no end to a season, garlic is planted as a matter of course in late autumn when the first frosts kick-start their tiny engine. Alluvial soil is just right for alliums so there'll always be at least half a bed devoted to garlic, one of the most important staples in our kitchen.

Leaf rust has done much to thwart our plans, and despite our religious crop rotation it always strikes at the beginning of June, literally the day after someone says, 'No sign of rust then this year?'

Fortunately this wind-borne virus doesn't kill garlic; it just knackers the leaves so that they can't photosynthesise. Once the leaves start looking like the Cor-Ten steel sculptures that might win you medals at the Chelsea Flower Show, it's time to pull them up as the bulbs just won't get any bigger.

Potash is meant to help prevent rust or at least slow it down by strengthening the tissues in the leaves, but with so much going on in April, May and June it's one job I keep forgetting to do. Overwatering doesn't help matters and this alone can ruin a crop completely, but bulbs won't swell sufficiently without some water during a dry spring so you have to gauge things carefully. I accidently left the hose on the garlic during the very dry spring of 2010 and this almost certainly accelerated the effect of rust, not to mention causing some bulbs to simply rot away. Foolish.

Sow: October–November or February–March, approx. 7cm deep.

Spacing: 15cm apart in rows 20cm apart.

Harvest: From mid-June.

Quantity: We plant a minimum of 50 bulbs; 100 bulbs will keep us going until late

Rust on Garlic

Globe artichoke

Jerusalem artichoke

winter.

Note: Cut off developing flower heads to divert all the plant's energy into the bulb.

Varieties: 'Early Wight'; 'Mediterranean'; 'Picardy Wight'; 'Thermidrome'.

Globe artichoke (*Cynara scolymus*)

My experience of growing globe artichokes has led me to distrust some seed companies as twice they have turned out to be cardoons. Not a complete disaster as the stem of the cardoon is edible.

Sow: February–March under cover.

Plant out: Late May.

Spacing: Approx. 80cm–1m apart.

Harvest: June onwards, when heads are still tight and not in flower.

Quantity: A couple of plants would be enough for us.

Note: While this is a permanent crop, it's best to renew plants every five years or so.

Varieties: 'Romanesco'; 'Violetto'.

Jerusalem artichoke (*Helianthus tuberosus*)

OK, let's get the toilet humour out of the way first. Jerusalem artichokes can make you fart. If you've got away so far without hearing them called fartichokes, I'm sorry to be the one to resort to puerile prose to bring it to your attention but, while we're on the subject, I've noticed that not everybody seems to be affected and even those who are might experience differing levels of intensity. A meal that starts with Jerusalem artichoke soup is always tainted with a little trepidation as to just who will be affected and to what degree. We see it as a sort of gastronomic Russian roulette and therefore choose our guests carefully if Jerusalem artichoke soup is on the menu.

Don't even think of buying this unless you're after a specific variety as anyone you can find growing it will only be too happy to let you have a few tubers.

Sow: January–March direct, 15cm deep.

Spacing: 60cm.

Harvest: October–March.

Quantity: A handful of tubers will eventually produce more than we need.

Note: Leave some tubers in the ground for next year.

Variety: 'Fuseau'.

Kale (*Brassica oleracea* var. *acephala*)

For years I struggled with the distinctive kale 'Cavolo Nero'. Not the growing of it, that bit's relatively easy, but in the kitchen. Its fleur-de-lys foliage belies the fact that it can be as tough as a milkman's satchel. However, it has earned a place at our plot more for its aesthetic appeal than its taste. The plants are a stunning focal point for any allotment, holding their beautiful form deep into winter, and with allotments always in a state of flux this alone merits growing them.

Sow: March–August.

Plant out: April–September.
Spacing: 60cm.
Harvest: June–February.
Quantity: Four to six plants are enough for us.
Note: When cooking, take out the central stem and boil it hard before adding a splash of olive oil, minced garlic and a little chilli to taste.
Varieties: 'Cavolo Nero' or 'Nero di Toscana'; 'Red Russian'; 'Red Ursa'.

Land cress (*Barbarea verna*)

Ideal for a cool shady part of the garden that doesn't dry out too much. The smaller leaves still pack a punch and will self-seed (not in a bad way) to keep you supplied with a useful leaf salad.
Sow: March–August direct, 2.5cm deep.
Spacing: 15–18cm apart.
Harvest: Early sowing from June, late sowings from November.
Quantity: A row or 10 plants is about as much as we've ever grown.
Note: Land cress is a member of the brassica family and ought to be rotated to prevent the likelihood of clubroot.

Leeks (*Allium ampeloprasum* var. *porrum*)

My all-time favourite perhaps. Not just because leeks are so versatile in the kitchen and can make your allotment look good in the depths of winter, but also because of the slightly bonkers technique involved in transplanting the seedlings, which, for some reason, makes you look as if you know what you're doing.

Seeds are sown in April either in a pot or, for better results, directly into the soil. When they reach pencil thickness by June (ours never really get that thick so I don't think this is crucial) they are dug up and the leaves and roots are cut by half before being replanted in a hole and submerged in water. Hacking them to within an inch of their lives like this sounds cruel, but that's what the books tell you and our leeks have always done well on it. Some think that it reduces transpiration and encourages a

Kale

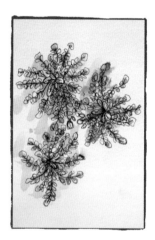

ABOVE Land cress
BELOW Leeks and seedlings

more fibrous root system before the plants have to worry about producing more leaves . . . others say that it just makes life easier when it comes to transplanting.

Some try and spoil the fun by saying that it makes no difference whatsoever. I did try planting alternate rows of trimmed and untrimmed, and I think there was a slight difference between the two. Typically, though, I can't remember which row was which, rendering the whole experiment redundant.

Sow: February–April (early sowings under cover, later sowings direct).

Plant out: June–July.

Spacing: 15cm apart in rows or blocks.

Harvest: October–May.

Quantity: We grow at least ten 3m rows and there is little if any wastage.

Note: Apart from keeping them weed-free to minimise the likelihood of rust, leeks have been perhaps the easiest and most reliable staple for even the brownest-fingered gardener at Bushy Park allotments . . . until now. Please welcome *Acrolepiopsis assectella*, commonly known as leek moth. Our crop, in the year of writing this book, has been severely affected with brown or pink streaks caused by the caterpilllars feeding within the leaves. Fleece will be used to stop the adult moth laying its eggs on this year's seedlings.

Varieties: 'Bleu de Solaise'; 'Musselburgh'; 'St Victor'.

Lemon verbena (*Aloysia triphylla*)

A desert island herb if ever there was one. The potency of the aroma from its leaves is so strong it's like smelling lemon concentrate and they make one of the most refreshing tisanes. I'm not a lover of herbal teas but Jekka McVicar has encouraged us to experiment with this herb, and we reckon an equal mix of lemon verbena, rosemary and mint is about as good as it gets in herbal-tea-world.

Note: While the plant may survive in a warm sheltered spot, it will stand more of a chance if kept in an unheated greenhouse. Prune back in spring when the first leaves appear.

Lettuce (*Lactuca sativa*)

Lettuces are always a little risky at our plot unless they are grown in modules first to give them a fighting chance. Some are even grown just in containers as back up.

ABOVE Lemon verbena
BELOW Lettuce

The best crops are from earlier sowings in cooler weather as they are less likely to bolt. Charles Dowding has taught us to stretch out the harvest period by picking the lower leaves of different plants rather than pulling up a whole plant. Less waste, more variety.

Sow: February–September (early sowings under cover).

Plant out: April–October.

Spacing: Varies with size. Check instructions on seed packet.

Harvest: Year round.

Quantity: One 3m row is usually enough.

Note: Successional sowing will give you leaves for most of the year. Lettuces don't mind a little shade, especially during the hottest months.

Varieties: 'Little Gem'; 'Lollo Rossa'; 'Pablo'; 'Red Iceberg'.

Onion (*Allium cepa*)

A problem vegetable for me if I'm honest. Most are grown from sets. In some years they are barely bigger than sets when I lift them several months later. I keep meaning to grow from seed but the lazy in me chooses sets every time. It's either a fertility thing or something to do with my timing but, with onions being so cheap to buy and with no discernible difference in taste, I've decided not to grow them any more and to free up space for other veg instead.

Sow: Seeds or sets March–April direct, and September–October for overwintering varieties.

Spacing: Onions don't like competition so expect smaller onions when planted 10cm apart rather than 20cm apart.

Harvest: May–October.

Quantity: Until now we've planted around 100 sets.

Note: Bend leaves over when they turn yellow to allow the bulb to ripen.

Varieties: 'Radar' (overwintering); 'Red Baron' (red); 'Sturon'.

Onions

Parsley (*Petroselinum crispum* var. *crispum*)

Curly leafed parsley is one of the few vegetables I have ever been able to give to Ted. He grows pretty much everything but is occasionally short of parsley and thyme. It's not a leaf that I liked much as a child. As an adult, too, I've been fairly indifferent to it but have become almost obsessive about its fresh taste since growing our own.

Sow: Direct or in modules in March.

Spacing: 15cm.

Harvest: From June or when there are enough leaves to pick from.

Quantity: Two 3m rows keep us in good supply with a bit extra to give away.

Note: For the freshest leaves, replant each year even if it survives the winter.

Varieties: Curly leafed parsley; Italian flat-leafed parsley (*Petroselinum crispum* var. *neapolitanum*).

Parsley

Parsnip (*Pastinaca sativa*)

Parsnips, like carrots, can be tricky. Fresh, reliable seed will readily germinate. It may take a little longer than you'd like but it will if you're patient. The trouble is that the seeds germinate just as slugs and snails are coming out of hibernation so either get quickly grazed or lost among emerging weeds. A dryish spring gives you a head start, and if you can get them to develop their first true leaves then you will almost certainly get a crop. Leave one or two in the ground and not only will you get some of the most beautiful flowers on the planet the following season but you'll be able to collect the seed to use the season after that. [1]

Sow: March–May direct.

Parsnips

---

[1] I'm a sucker for umbellifers and the humble parsnip is one of the best. Buttercup-yellow umbels flower from mid-May to late June, which makes it an ideal candidate for the Chelsea Flower Show. I can't remember anyone using it there. At the time of writing I am preparing to make a show garden there for the *Telegraph* in 2011 and have potted up most of our parsnips in the hope that they will be a key feature in my plant palette.

Parsnip flower

Spacing: 15cm apart in rows 30cm apart.

Harvest: September–March.

Quantity: Two rows of 3m are more than enough.

Note: They will self-seed freely if allowed and, depending on where they land, can either be left to flower or be pulled up and used in the kitchen when young and tender.

Varieties: 'Tender and True'; 'White Gem'.

Pea *(Pisum sativum)*

Something I mull over from time to time is the number of peas that must be grown in the world to keep the frozen pea industry going. The frozen ones aren't at all bad either, making us question why we try and grow them on our plot in the first place. Pick and taste them fresh from the pod and you'll understand. The peas that we grow are treats, sweets if you like, that we snack on at any time during marathon days at the plot. Rarely do we go home with enough of them to make a meal. Give it a try but get into the habit of successional sowing to give you a long harvest. Our experience is a bit hit-and-miss unless we grow them to a decent size in pots and train them up birch or hazel sticks to make sure they are well out of harm's way when they go into the ground. Later sowings, directly into the soil, always fall prey to slugs, who appreciate them too.

Sow: February–May.

Spacing: 15cm apart in rows 75cm apart.

Plant out: May–June.

Harvest: May–October.

Quantity: We grow two rows of 3m but can never really get enough.

Notes: Some people like to soak their peas in paraffin to put mice off the scent. I've

Peas

never tried it. Early and late crops will outwit the pea moth caterpillar, which is active during July.

Varieties: 'Alderman'; 'Delikata' (mangetout variety); 'Hatif d'Annonay'; 'Hurst Green Shaft'; 'Serpette Guilloteau'.

Potato (*Solanum tuberosum*)

Our sandy loam is really not the best soil for potatoes, especially for my favourite King Edwards, which require more moisture than most, but cooking new potatoes at the allotment within minutes of digging them up is one of those life-affirming moments when everything seems just right with the world.

Encouraging buds by 'chitting' potatoes gives them a head start. Rubbing all but the strongest pair of buds is said to increase the size of potatoes.

Most books tell you to plant your potatoes and draw up ('earth-up') the soil over the leaves as they grow (a) to protect them from frost and (b) to allow more tubers to be formed up the stem. This is fine except I generally see people 'earthing-up' as soon as they plant their spuds. This looks all very neat and tidy but for a plant that thrives on moisture – producing 30 per cent more spuds than when left unwatered – wouldn't it make sense to plant the spuds in a furrow? This would channel rainwater to where it was needed and eventually allow more of the stem to be earthed up, significantly increasing yield. A generous layer of newspaper and organic matter in the trench will also retain moisture.

The Portuguese at our allotment, many from Madeira, practise good farming techniques and this is often the way they plant their potatoes. Common sense really. A reminder not to take everything you read as gospel.

While a range of potatoes have been grown over the years, we tend to concentrate on 1st earlies and 2nd earlies more than on maincrop varieties, which have a more difficult time with slugs and are more susceptible to blight. 'Winston', 'Belle de Fontenay' and 'Charlotte' are favourites. 'Maris Piper' is one maincrop that seems to cope reasonably with our alluvial soil and we always like 'Ratte' or 'Pink Fir Apple' for their novelty and nuttiness.

Sow: February–April direct, approx. 10–15cm deep.

Spacing: Early varieties, 30cm apart in rows 50cm apart. Maincrop varieties, 35cm apart in rows 70cm apart.

Harvest: May–October.

Quantity: One 3m × 3m raised bed is usually devoted to potatoes and more where we can fit them in. We generally run out of stock by the end of January.

Note: Potatoes should be 'chitted' from late January. Place the tubers in trays with 'eyes' uppermost in a cool, light, frost-free place. The shoots should be around 2cm long when ready for planting.

Varieties: 'Belle de Fontenay'; 'Charlotte'; 'Kestrel'; 'King Edward'; 'Maris Piper'; 'Pink Fir Apple'; 'Ratte'; 'Winston'.

Radish (*Raphanus sativus*)

Radishes are so quick and easy to grow that they are a useful crop for beginners keen

Radishes

to see the results of their labours. They are also particularly useful as a catch crop, something that can be grown quickly when there is a temporary bare patch in the vegetable plot.

Some people like their radishes hot; I prefer the milder varieties which don't repeat on you so much. The best way of finding out what you like is to experiment.

The Austrian cooking radish ('Weiner Runder Kohlschwarzer'), as supplied by The Real Seed Catalogue, is more like a swede or a turnip than a radish. Their black textured skin makes them a bit of an oddity but they are a useful bonus to harvest in winter. Sow these in July and harvest from November to February.

Sow: March–September direct.

Spacing: 3cm apart in rows 15cm apart or scatter liberally in a vacant patch.

Harvest: Four to six weeks after planting. Don't let them get too woody.

Quantity: One 3m row at any given time is more than enough.

Note: Keep watered for sustained growth. If some escape your attention and set seed, the young pods can be thrown into a salad for a crunchy contrast.

Varieties: 'French Breakfast' is a reliable sort; 'Cherry Belle'; 'Red Top'.

Rhubarb

Rhubarb (*Rheum rhaponticum*)

A large clump of rhubarb underneath a medlar tree at the front of our plot obligingly feeds us in early spring, a very lean time of the year. The variety is unknown, possibly 'Victoria', but it reliably sends up chunky stalks from March onwards. New varieties have been planted elsewhere as this clump has been in the same place for almost a decade and may soon decide to retire.

Forget seed, it takes far too long. Buy as a ready grown plant from a garden centre or, if you know someone who has an established clump, ask them to give you a slice of the crown in the dormant season. It's a permanent crop which will stay put for a decade or so, and therefore needs good fertile soil with plenty of compost added to give it a head start, but allow it to settle for a season before you start cropping.

Sow: Plant crowns in December.

Spacing: Depends on variety but approx. 1m.

Harvest: From April, when stalks are big enough.

Rocket

Quantity: Three clumps at our plot keep us, and our neighbours, reasonably well fed.

Note: The leaves of rhubarb are toxic and should not be eaten.

Varieties: 'Champagne'; 'Coutts Red Stick'; 'Seedling Piggot'; 'Victoria'.

Rocket (*Rucola coltivata*)

Wild rocket (*Diplotaxis tenuifolia*) self-seeds at our plot and so is available much of the year. Salad rocket is grown too. Both varieties have a more peppery taste than the overpriced, measly sprig you buy in the shops (don't ask me why) but salad rocket has the edge. Use it to perk up a salad or add it fresh (not cooked) to decorate a piping hot pizza.

Sow: March–September direct.

Spacing: Sow randomly where there is space (you can't have too much of it) but if you are desperate for rows then 30cm apart will do.

Harvest: April–November.

Quantity: We dot this around wherever there is space but in essence it probably amounts to one 3m row.

Note: Both types will overwinter nicely in a cold greenhouse, polytunnel or cloche.

Runner bean (*Phaseolus coccineus*)

We've grown fewer runner beans of late, having been seduced by their French cousins. However, while writing this book, Kathy (our neighbouring plot-holder) gave us seedlings of 'White Lady', which turned out to be virtually stringless and delicious. It was also vigorous enough to make it to the top of our tallest wigwam so it kept us in good supply all summer, though we needed a ladder to pick them. Feed the soil well before planting and, if you're plagued with slugs, grow them on in pots first to give them a good head start.

Sow: April–June under cover or April–May direct.

Plant out: May–July.

Spacing: 25cm apart.

Harvest: June–October.

Quantity: One of our three-legged wigwams with three plants growing up each leg is plenty.

Note: Borage (*Borago officinalis*) or *Verbena bonariensis* planted nearby will help attract bees which, in turn, will help pollinate the runner beans. A late sowing is always useful to give you beans well into early autumn.

Varieties: 'Pole Star'; 'Scarlet Emperor'; 'Streamline'; 'White Lady'.

Runner beans

Salsify (*Tragopogon porrifolius*) and Scorzonera (*Scorzonera hispanica*)

Salsify and scorzonera are nomads and pretty flowering ones too. The purple flowers of salsify and yellow of scorzonera are one way of telling them apart above ground. The root of salsify is lighter in colour than scorzonera but there's hardly any difference in taste.

They'll self-seed in the tightest spot, making them difficult to harvest, so it's worth sowing a line or two to make life easier. Both are said to taste like oysters but, having never eaten an oyster, I don't feel qualified to comment.

Boiled, baked or sautéed in butter, they make a delicious and unusual treat.

Sow: April–May direct.

Spacing: 15cm.

Harvest: October–November.

Quantity: Two 3m rows (one of each).

Salsify

Shallot

Spinach

Sprouting broccoli

Note: The roots are more delicate than carrots or parsnips so take care when harvesting.

Varieties: Salsify – 'Giant'; 'Mammoth'. Scorzonera – 'Russian Giant'.

Shallot (*Allium cepa* var. *aggregatum*)

Shallots are brilliant for beginners. With onions, you plant one onion set and get one onion back, usually bigger but, as I've pointed out on our plot, not that much bigger. With shallots, however, you get at least five bulbs back for every one. It's the same family as onion obviously, but a much better and more reliable deal all round from our perspective. Their size makes them appear fiddly to use in the kitchen but think whole, halved, roasted and braised and it will open up new avenues of gastronomy to explore.

Sow: February–March, seed under cover or sets direct.

Spacing: 20cm apart in rows 30cm apart.

Harvest: July–September.

Quantity: Our two 3m rows are never enough.

Note: Let the sun dry the bulbs for a few days before storing.

Varieties: 'Pikant'; 'Red Sun'.

Spinach (*Spinacia oleracea*)

Spinach is a favourite of ours but when faced with an army of hungry slugs in spring we usually defer to chard or perpetual spinach. The texture is more delicate and young spinach leaves are a real treat in a salad bowl. Regular (not excessive) watering gives best results.

Sow: March–October direct.

Spacing: 20cm apart in rows 30cm apart.

Harvest: Year round.

Quantity: Two 3m rows are good but we could use more.

Note: New Zealand spinach (*Tetragonia expansa*) is a similar leaf vegetable valued for its resistance to bolting.

Spinach varieties: 'Matador' (summer); 'Dominant' (autumn, winter).

Sprouting broccoli (*Brassica oleracea* var. *italica*)

When I eventually allowed my sprouting broccoli enough time in the ground to set their florets, I was confused as to why they were so much thinner than the fat heads you see at the grocers. It turned out that what we called broccoli in the shops is in fact calabrese. The thinner (and more delicious) florets we now know as 'sprouting broccoli' and the season wouldn't be complete without it.

While you can grow several varieties to give you broccoli from summer till the following spring, we mostly grow the purple, late-sprouting varieties which provide a lifeline when little else is on offer at the plot in April. They have a delicacy which is very welcome at that time of year and are eaten daily in healthy stir-fries.

Sow: April–June under cover although can be sown direct.

Plant out: June–July.

For a second, Christine thought she was going to have to use the epitaph, 'He was squashed', when the large pumpkin in the above picture (top right) rolled off the roof and missed my head by a millimetre.

Spacing: Approx 60cm between each plant.
Harvest: July–May.
Quantity: Four plants are usually enough for us.
Note: Wider spacings increase the yield of each plant.
Varieties: 'Rudolph' (early); 'Crown and Sceptre'; 'Late Purple Sprouting'.

Squash (*Cucurbita maxima*)

Squash

We have grown pumpkins in the past but find squash more practical and less wasteful. Squash plays an important part in our diet and just a few will keep us fed throughout winter and occasionally into spring.

They can take up a lot of space and sprawl over anything in their path, but smaller varieties can also be trained to grow vertically on wigwams or plant supports – an invaluable growing technique where space is tight.

It's always a surprise to see a plant supporting a heavy gourd that might weigh in excess of two kilos. Some inadvertently end up adding extra support to our hazel wigwams by enveloping the poles.

It's quite possible to tire of these by late winter but we always grow at least three different varieties to keep the larder well stocked for winter. They need a long growing season so get them into the ground just as soon as the weather looks like behaving.
Sow: March–May under cover.
Plant out: June–July.
Spacing: 1m.
Harvest: October–November.
Quantity: Three plants should be sufficient in a good year with lots of sun.
Note: They are the greediest of vegetables so feed well with well-rotted compost and liquid manure. Cut leaves away from the fruit to let the sun ripen the skin and improve its ability to store well.
Varieties: 'Blue Hubbard'; 'Butternut'; 'Marina di Chioggia'; 'Uchiki Kuri'. 'Jack Be Little' and other smaller varieties are good, too, especially where space is a problem.

Swede

Swede (*Brassica napus* var. *napobrassica*)

We don't care for turnips (which is why I haven't included them in this list) but we love swede and always feel ridiculously proud when we bring one home to the kitchen. It's hardly the most aesthetically pleasing of vegetables, but just the thought of swede steamed and mashed with a huge knob of butter is enough to prepare you for the worst winter can throw at you.
Sow: April–June direct.
Spacing: 20cm apart in rows 30cm apart.
Harvest: October–February.
Quantity: Two 3m rows are only just enough.
Note: Keep weed free and water regularly. Leaves can be steamed as greens.
Varieties: 'Champion Red Top'; 'Joan'.

Sweetcorn (*Zea mays*)

Like peas, the taste of sweetcorn eaten within minutes of the cob being picked is incomparable to anything you'll ever buy. Sugars won't have changed into starch so the cob needs minimal cooking and can even be eaten raw if you catch it right.

The success of our sweetcorn largely depends on the squirrels that live in the trees adjacent to our plot and how meticulous we have been in netting the corn in the first place.

Dhundi Raj gave us maize from Nepal but this turned out to be forage maize for feeding cattle and, despite its size (growing to around 2.5m), needed more weeks of sun than this island can provide to fully ripen.

Sow: April under cover, May direct.

Plant out: May–June.

Spacing: 30cm each way in blocks to aid pollination (which is by wind, not insects).

Harvest: Late August–September/October.

Quantity: We grow a block of around 25 plants, which is sufficient.

Note: Leaves on the cobs keep them fresh, so don't strip them off until you're ready to eat them.

Varieties: 'Double Standard'; 'Kelvedon Glory' (F1); 'Sweet Nugget' (F1).

Sweetcorn

Tomato (*Lycopersicon esculentum*)

One of my first jobs on leaving school was at a Thames Water sewerage plant near Sandown racecourse. Not the most salubrious introduction to full-time employment but I remember being fascinated by the tomato plants colonising embankments where sterilised waste had been piled. The resilience of a tomato seed that can still germinate

Tomatoes

after 27 feet of colon and miles of pipeline has to be admired.

I was never really fond of tomatoes until we grew our own. Even then much depends on how they've been grown. Those raised outside are generally happier and tastier and, in a hot summer, pure Mediterranean. The risk is that damp weather will bring blight but it's definitely worth having a try.

Our inexperience with veg growing is usually revealed when it comes to our greenhouse tomatoes. Erratic watering and, occasionally, poor ventilation always leads to a certain amount of blossom drop so they never fulfil their potential. Outside, as long as there is plenty of sunshine to keep blight away, they fare much better.

Gauging how much water tomatoes need depends on the weather. A hot sunny day might warrant two litres of water whereas a cool, cloudy day barely more than a quarter of a litre. Overwatering can also dilute the taste of tomatoes, so don't be tempted to water too much as they ripen. A hose or plastic bottle dug into the soil will encourage roots to grow deep. Shallower roots benefit from a liquid feed once or twice a week. We use Maxicrop or comfrey liquid, the latter rendering the greenhouse an offence to the olfactory senses for several hours afterwards.

I appreciate that this isn't much help, so I would urge you to have a look at Mark Diacono's book, *Veg Patch*, for a better understanding of the complexities involved in the taste and growing of tomatoes.

Sow: February–March under cover.

Plant out: May–June for outdoor varieties.

Spacing: 60cm.

Harvest: July–October.

Quantity: We usually grow eight plants in the greenhouse and the same outside. This keeps us well stocked with liittle waste as they can be cooked into sauce and frozen.

Note: Pick green tomatoes in October before the first frost to ripen on a windowsill at home.

Varieties: 'Black Russian' (or 'Purple Ukraine'); 'Costoluto Genovese'; 'Gardener's Delight'; 'Latah'; 'Rose de Berne'.

Length of time seed can be kept in a cool, dry place

1 year	2 years	3 years	5 years	6 years	7 years
Parsnip	Carrot	Beetroot	Lettuce	Bean	Tomato
	Onion	Brassicas		Pea	
	Leek	Spinach			
	Parsley	Sweetcorn			

Monthly tasks

January
- Clear weeds.
- Mulch with well-rotted compost.
- Check tools.
- Use cloches or fleece to warm the soil.
- Plan a planting strategy and keep a written record for future reference.
- Place orders for seeds.
- Plant fruit trees, bushes and canes.
- Prune fruit trees/bushes and check tree ties.
- Lift and divide rhubarb. Mulch around existing crowns.
- Inspect stored crops and discard spoilt ones.
- Begin chitting potatoes in a light, cool (frost-free) environment away from direct sun.

February
- Continue digging and conditioning soil.
- Apply fertiliser to asparagus beds.
- Prepare trenches for runner beans (45cm deep and fill with organic matter including weeds and veg waste.
- Disinfect pots/trays/greenhouses – organic disinfectant – Citrox/www.citrox.net
- Lift and divide rhubarb. Mulch around existing crowns.
- Check debris (hiding places for slugs) and remove from garden.
- Inspect stored crops.
- Continue chitting potatoes in a light cool environment away from direct sun.
- Plant fruit trees/bushes and mulch well with compost.
- Prune fruit trees/bushes and check tree ties.

March
- Still time to prepare ground by digging (unless using no-dig method) and adding well-rotted compost except where alliums and umbellifers are being planted.
- Clean pots/trays, etc.
- Weed between crops.
- Earth up potatoes in pots and protect with fleece if necessary.

- Lift last parsnips unless saving for seed.
- Lift and divide rhubarb. Mulch around existing crowns.
- Continue tidying and searching for slugs and snails.
- Protect fruit trees/bushes from frost and think about and start pest control as aphids begin to appear in April.
- Last chance to plant bare root fruit trees/bushes.

April
- Prepare ground for sowing and weed and mulch if warm.
- Stake and support peas.
- Prepare tomato beds – dig over and add manure and compost.
- Earth up early potatoes and those in pots.
- Clear last brassica stumps.
- Take offsets from globe artichokes.
- Green manures that can be sown on unused ground up to August: mustard, crimson clover, fenugreek, buckwheat, phacelia, alfalfa.

May
- Weed, water and clear debris.
- Prepare ground for veg to be planted out from sowings under cover.
- Stake/support beans.
- Protect from pests – carrot fly, blackfly, cabbage root fly and flea beetle. Enviromesh available from www.agralan.co.uk (01285 860015).
- Earth up early and maincrop potatoes.
- Thin crops such as beetroot, carrots, etc.
- Successional sowings of salad leaves.

June

- Weed, mulch and hoe.
- Clear garden, keep debris to a minimum and reduce pests.
- Protect fruit/brassicas from birds: www.knowlenets.co.uk (01308 424342).
- Stake and support plants.
- Thin apples after June drop.
- Protect carrots against carrot fly (see May).
- Water seedlings.
- Earth up potatoes.
- Regularly harvest crops to create a steady supply.

July

- Weed, hoe, mulch and water. Little and often.
- Damp down greenhouses.
- Check for pests and diseases – potato and tomato blight, cabbage caterpillars.
- Remove dead/diseased debris.
- Harvest, dry and store garlic and shallots.
- Freeze excess broad beans.
- Dig up potatoes.
- Remove side shoots from cordon tomatoes.

August

- Weed, hoe, mulch and water.
- Harvest and clear the ground.
- Stake and support plants.
- Check for pests and diseases – potato and tomato blight, cabbage caterpillars.
- Dig up potatoes and store.
- Cut away squash and pumpkin leaves to help ripen.
- Dry and store onions.
- Harvest beans often to encourage more flowers.

September

- Hoe and weed.
- Harvest, clear ground and clear debris.
- Stake and secure plants.
- Remove yellowing foliage from brassicas.
- Cut down asparagus ferns.
- Watch out for pests – caterpillars on brassicas, slugs.

- Allow sun to ripen skins of pumpkin and squash before storing.
- Store all other crops.
- Sow green manure: winter-grazing rye, winter tares.

October

- Clear debris, hoe and weed.
- Protect plants from frost – mulch, fleece, cloches.
- Lift and store crops for winter.
- Let the last outdoor tomatoes ripen under cloches.
- Begin cleaning up and mulching with compost.
- Clear Jerusalem artichokes, especially invasive tubers.

November

- Clear debris, hoe and weed, especially under cloches.
- Protect plants from frost with mulch, fleece or cloches.
- Lift and store crops for winter.
- Clean greenhouse and tools.
- Continue clearing and mulching.
- Remove dying leaves on brassicas and inspect for slugs.
- Lift and divide rhubarb. Mulch around existing crowns.

December

- Continue to hoe, weed and mulch.
- Lift and store crops for winter.
- Lift and divide rhubarb. Mulch around existing crowns.
- Clean greenhouse and tools.
- Remove dying leaves on brassicas and inspect for slugs.
- Support Brussels sprouts if necessary.
- Enjoy being self-sufficient for Christmas dinner!

CHAPTER SIX

Flowers and fruit

Flowers have always been part of allotment culture.

Flowers have always been part of allotment culture. Cutting flowers in particular and traditionally chrysanthemums and dahlias. You still see them now but a general shift in the sort of people who tend the plots, together with a wide interest in biodiversity and more appreciation of the leisure side of allotments, means that a much broader palette of flowers is being used.

As I'm a garden designer I find that plants left over from projects occasionally find their way to the allotment, either as temporary guests or as permanent residents. Herbs, being so versatile, are increasingly popular and we have explored their potential in the border at the front of our plot where the soil is at its leanest. Box and yew provide some structure, betraying either a designer instinct to create a 'garden' or a need to evoke a sense of order, which can be particularly useful when weeds are getting the upper hand.

For those new to gardening bear in mind that weeding often goes unappreciated. When I first started gardening in the mid-1980s, customers rarely noticed all the hours of work that went into weeding borders but instantly admired and appreciated a mown lawn or neatly trimmed hedge, which had invariably taken just a few minutes. I soon learned to cut lawns and hedges the minute a client popped out for a while, knowing that even if I'd been inclined to sunbathe until they got back they would be suitably impressed by all the hard work that had taken place while they were out.

Allium

Flowers

Allium

Onions, chives (*Allium schoenoprasum*) and garlic (*A. sativum*) we grow for the plate, but the globular form, their ornamental cousins, are much valued for their contribution to the herb border. *Allium aflatuense* 'Purple Sensation', *A. christophii* and *A. schubertii* are the most obvious statements in early summer, while *A. sphaerocephalon* perpetuates the display with their edible-looking (though sadly not) flowers and bloated straw-coloured seedheads. Despite a tendency to be invasive, wild garlic (*A. ursinum*) is something we ought to try in shadier parts of the plot as the leaves make a delicious soup.

Borage *(Borago officinalis)*

Borage flowers frozen in ice cubes have become the quintessential complement in a glass of Pimms on a hot summer's day. It's one of those simple ideas that will

Borage

impress your guests out of all proportion to the effort it takes. The flowers can also be crystalised (a fiddly job by all accounts and not one for chubby fingers) to decorate cakes and the leaves can also be used in the kitchen. There is so much going for this plant that it feels mean to weed it out of the herb bed and elsewhere in the plot where it has self-seeded. But left to its own devices it will smother neighbouring plants so be ruthless when it starts taking advantage. It's easy to pull out at any stage but catch it young before it flowers and the leaves can be used for salad or soup. Excessive use of this herb can cause liver damage and some people may experience contact dermatitis, but this Mediterranean beauty is delightful in any garden.

California poppy (*Eschscholzia californica*)

These delightful poppies appeared from nowhere one year and have remained with us ever since. From June they brighten up the herb bed and anywhere else they can self-seed, each one a miniature shining sun of joy. Much daintier than the opium poppy, which asserts itself as the 'daddy' on our plot, their splash of the freshest orange is almost enough to quench a thirst.

Evening primrose (*Oenothera biennis*)

Another self-seeder and a little too big really for the plot but always a welcome sight in late summer. We'll always leave a token few and take a draught of its perfume just before returning home as a reward for working late. A smaller, more delicate variety, *Oenothera odorata* 'Sulphurea', has been planted so that we can get to know it and provide nectar for moth pollinators.

Fennel (*Foeniculum vulgare*)

Common fennel is indispensible at the plot with its frothy foliage on zigzag stems, topped with perfect landing-pad umbellifers for hoverflies and other insects. The culinary variety (*F. vulgare* var. *azoricum*) is grown for the bulb (see page 75) but the leaves and seeds of both varieties are edible.

Forget-me-not (*Myosotis sylvatica*)

While the colonising, nomadic qualities of the forget-me-not are to be admired, I've never wanted to encourage it at the allotment. It has the knack of getting around in a rather discreet and charming way, bringing cushions of sky to ground. Christine has always had more time for it and is happy for it to be as cheeky as it likes, brightening things up in April and early May when the plot is at its least productive.

The plant is genuinely uplifting and it seems brutal to dig it up in its prime, but it takes up a surprising amount of space in a vegetable garden, let alone providing shelter for slugs, so I adopted a more ruthless approach the year before writing this book in an effort to regain the upper hand.

On visiting the plot a week or two after my mother died, it was as poignant as it gets to see this potent symbol of tragic love more abundant than ever before. Great swathes billowed from parts of the plot where it had never been seen. The plot was mourning the passing of a friend. The inclination to dig them up to make space for

seed sowing was instantly replaced by a need to let them sing and dance far and wide as if to proclaim our loss to the whole wide world.

Love-in-a-mist (*Nigella damascena*)

Love-in-a-mist, like borage, is a classic self-seeder and one that must be watched. Like borage it also carries blue flowers, a useful attribute for any flower in a veg plot as the colour is very attractive to bees. Unlike the spice, black cumin (*Nigella sativa*), it has no edible qualities but we leave it to flower where it seeds around the plot, especially on the paths where it provides a cool place for slugs to hide during the day, making it easier for us to find them.

Mistletoe (*Viscum album*)

An orchard I have come to know and love is in the village of North Wootton in Somerset where New Year's Eve is celebrated with a roaring bonfire, mulled cider and close family. Each year I bring a sprig of mistletoe from North Wootton orchard back to our plot and plug nicks and cracks in my apple trees with its sticky seed to see if I can propagate this fabled symbol of Yuletide romance. Recently, on winter pruning a Bramley at the back of the plot, I was chuffed (actually quietly ecstatic and a little smug if I'm honest) to find a healthy stem of mistletoe that must have sprouted leaves a year or two before I noticed it. We now have a link between two locations, both loved, both productive and both resonating with memories, customs, events and stories that make each place so individual, so special.

LEFT FROM TOP California poppies; Evening primrose; Fennel; Forget-me-not
ABOVE Like borage, the blue flowers of nigella are especially attractive to insects. Provided they don't get too cheeky, we let them self seed in and around the raised beds, especially where beans are to be sown.
RIGHT Mistletoe

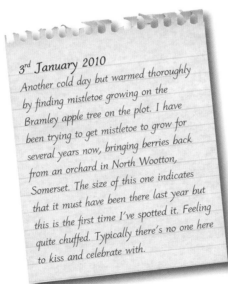

3rd January 2010
Another cold day but warmed thoroughly by finding mistletoe growing on the Bramley apple tree on the plot. I have been trying to get mistletoe to grow for several years now, bringing berries back from an orchard in North Wootton, Somerset. The size of this one indicates that it must have been there last year but this is the first time I've spotted it. Feeling quite chuffed. Typically there's no one here to kiss and celebrate with.

The self-seeders here (poppy, nasturtium, parsnip, marigold, *Cerinthe major* and *Tulipa sprengeri*) appear to a greater or lesser degree, depending on how much of the soil is disturbed. The pitcher plants (*Sarracenia flava*) reside in the greenhouse for no other reason than that I like the look of them, but some think that it suggests latent carnivorous tendencies.

Opium poppy (*Papaver somniferum*)

Around the time I started writing this book I dug over the herb bed at the front of the plot. Soil disturbance often gives a chance for seeds that have lain dormant for years to flourish, and in this case we were amazed when a gorgeous red poppy that we'd never seen before exploited the gaps between newly planted herbs and gave a most dramatic display for us and a virtual swarm of bees to enjoy. Some had to be weeded out early so as to give the young herbs a chance, and once seed was set the stems were thinned again. It's amazing how something so transient can give so much joy and lasting memory.

Phlomis russeliana

A clump of this beautiful perennial (given to me by Gay Search, whose garden had been designed by Dan Pearson) is a permanent fixture by the Wonky Shed and threatens to colonise other parts of the plot through seed and fragments of root that have fallen from a wheelbarrow load of it bound for the compost heap. To call it a thug sounds rude but it is and it can suffocate other plants nearby if not checked every year, but its sculptural flowers and later seedheads are so striking that there'll always be a place for it somewhere. Chaffinches and goldfinches occasionally feed on the seedheads.

Verbena bonariensis

Having known this plant for fifteen years and used it in many private gardens, I often wonder why I don't tire of using it but it is always a welcome sight at the plot. Despite its uselessness in the kitchen it does benefit the plot not just by lifting the spirits but also because its delicate, sweet-scented corymbs, not unlike buddleia, are the magnet of magnets for pollinating insects, creating a heady haze at the height of summer. Its tall thin stems look delicate but are amazingly sturdy and are most obliging in allowing a view through so that they never really get in the way of anything. We dig up seedlings and give them to friends. They think we have given them treasure.

Fruit

Apples and pears (*Malus spp.* and *Pyrus spp.*)

The disappearance of the English orchard over the last century has been alarming. Each one grubbed up for development takes away something unique and peculiar to its locality, something that is the epitome of what is known as 'a sense of place'. The charity, Common Ground, has done much to halt the destruction by raising awareness and engendering pride in local distinctiveness, preserving orchards under threat and replanting them where they have been lost.

A small orchard in the community plot next door has been struggling to find its feet and it's completely my fault. Semi-dwarfing rootstock was used so that the trees wouldn't grow too large and shade neighbouring plots. In hindsight, as our soil is so poor, a slightly more vigorous rootstock would have been better.

The apples and pears on our plot, however, have flourished since the end of our

FROM TOP Opium poppy;
Phlomis russeliana;
Verbena bonariensis.

Apples and pears

second season when they were planted as a mark of our commitment. Two-year-old maidens planted and trained as espaliers were grown for three years before we let them fruit. Maidens often show willing to fruit straight away but it makes sense to pick all fruit off in the first two years so they can put all their energy into growing roots and a good framework of branches. Annoyingly, just as we picked our first harvest, I developed an allergy to various fruit including apples and pears. This is a major blow for someone who is mostly vegetarian, and I still can't resist eating them from time to time regardless of how much my mouth itches afterwards. The effect is slightly less severe with home-grown organic fruit, which makes me wonder whether commercial spraying has anything to do with it.

Despite this, the magic of apples and pears still has me captivated, and each year I try to find room for more so that between them there is a healthy mix of varieties. The danger is that they grow too high and cast shade over some of the beds. While a little shade can be a useful thing for some leaf salads, most of the new espaliers will be restricted to two or three tiers. The most recent order has been for cider apples. As each new fruit tree planted is another reason to commit a few more years to the plot, it's unlikely we will give up our plot until we've successfully brewed our few demijohns of scrumpy.

Varieties we grow:

Apples: 'Adam's Pearmain'; 'Api'; 'Crawley Beauty'; 'Court Pendu Plat'; 'Dabinett' (cider); 'D'Arcy Spice'; 'Duchess of Oldenburg'; 'Egremont Russet'; 'Karmijn de Sonnaville'; 'King of the Pippins'; 'Lane's Prince Albert'; 'Nettlestone Pippin'.

Pears: 'Black Worcester'; 'Conference'; 'Doyenne du Comice'; 'Josephine de Malines'; 'Louise Bon of Jersey'; 'Merton Pride'; 'Seckle'; 'Willams bon Chretien'.

Apricot (*Prunus armeniaca*)

An apricot tree is a beautiful tree on its own even without the fruit, and we have recently planted one close (and a little too close I think) to the quince. Not ideal but sometimes you just get carried away by the excitement of having your own fruit trees and you accept the consequences of less than uniform shapes. This is no bad thing and trees that have had to fight for airspace often look all the more interesting for it. We've planted 'Golden Glow', a dessert, self-fertile variety found on the side of the Malvern Hills in Worcestershire.

Apricot blossom

Blackberry (*Rubus fruticosus*)

The last allotment we took on was completely covered in blackberries. They did a good job of shading out the weeds but were eventually reduced to a more sensible patch on the boundary. We start cropping around the end of July, which always seems much too early, especially as there aren't by then any apples to join them in a pie. Many are given away, some are frozen, but there are still enough for children, birds and mice to snaffle too.

Blackcurrants (*Ribes nigrum*)

Blackcurrants are jewels of encapsulated childhood dreams. The metallic smell and sharp taste are so intense it's like a distillation of itself that virtually ruptures saliva glands, instantly transporting me to a time of adventure when the world was so much bigger and everything seemed just right. Blackcurrant jam is without doubt the easiest and most intoxicating you can make, the smell of it bubbling on the kitchen stove just too heady for words. I could get quite excited about blackcurrants.
Variety: 'Ben Lomond'.

Blackberries

Cape gooseberry (*Physalis peruviana*)

This fruit, a berry growing in a type of lantern encasement, may be something of a novelty, but as far as taste is concerned, it packs a real punch. Left in their husks, the berries can be stored for many weeks but, for us, they are too tempting a snack, especially when we have worked for hours at the plot without eating or drinking. Ours was grown from seed and spent a few months languishing in a pot before finding its way into the soil in a corner of the greenhouse where it obligingly produces a regular supply of berries from mid-summer to the first frost. Unsurprisingly (given that it is a member of the Solanaceae family) the taste is one or two steps beyond a very sweet tomato; it hovers tantalisingly short of full-blown dessert so it will be just as likely to find its way into a leaf salad as a meringue. While putting the final touches to this book I've noticed that our plant looks decidedly the worse for wear after the sustained cold snap around Christmas that froze everything solid in the greenhouse for weeks. If it dies we'll buy seed to grow more as it is quite undemanding and thrives on neglect.

Cape gooseberry

Fig (*Ficus carica*)

We're very tight-fisted when it comes to figs. I think we've only ever given away four (to Julie) and that was probably done begrudgingly. This is because figs are, quite simply,

There's a good argument for growing more permanent crops such as soft fruit to cut down on the amount of work needed to keep the plot in good shape.

Sunday 4th July 2010

My dad comes to the allotment for a couple of hours. He's not keen on gardening. In fact I'd go so far as to say that he hates it. His name is Vic and he is universally recognised as the personification of One Foot in the Grave's Victor Meldrew. Having already dragged him around the Hampton Court Flower Show, I'm pushing my luck by bringing him to the plot. Some might think it thoughtless to put him on gooseberry-picking duty while I pick blackcurrants, but my plan is that any job I get him to do after getting pricked and stabbed by the merciless gooseberry thorns will seem like heaven. Amazingly he doesn't complain but I can see his pain and eventually swap my almost full bowl of blackcurrants with his paltry collection of gooseberries. Less than five minutes go by before the words 'I don't believe it!' confirm my worst fear. He's dropped the bloody bowl. Knowing just how much I covet blackcurrants, he spends the next 20 minutes on his hands and knees picking them up one at a time from the earth. When he's done we decide to go home where it's relatively safe.

food of the gods. They are sweet, they are gooey, they are flagrantly sexy and the fig is a fine tree to boot. We planted a tree, of unknown variety, five years ago in front of the Wonky Shed where it gets full sun and, while it could never satiate our appetite, we harvest enough to make us feel, just for a moment, that we're in spitting distance of the Mediterranean. Ours has been planted in a hole lined with paving slabs as figs are meant to fruit more prolifically if their roots are restricted. Figs are capable of fruiting two or three times a year in warmer climates but only one crop a year can be expected in the UK. Some people have trouble getting their trees to bear decent quality fruit, usually because they expect the small figs that are left on the tree at the end of the summer to do their thing the following season. They won't. The figs that will mature the following summer are no bigger than a pea and are tucked into the leaf axils. Removing any fruit that looks like a fig in the autumn will allow the tree to pour its energy into these tiny bumps and allow them to develop without competition.

Fig

Greengage (*Prunus domestica*)

Greengages have a nuttier and sweeter flavour than plums, a flavour that is thankfully imparted and accentuated with jam-making. We have two trees on the plot and the plan was to fan train them. Espaliers I can cope with, but fans involve too much thinking for me and, as a consequence, the two trees have escaped their confines and are about to become trees in their own right. The downside is that there really isn't enough room for two of them and one will have to go, even though they are reliable pollinators for each other. The dilemma will be which one. Original labels have long since disappeared. The one with larger, juicier fruit is definitely more of a dessert gage; the other is smaller, no less tasty but with a firmer texture which is excellent for jam. It might take a decade to make such a decision.

Greengage

Gooseberry (*Ribes grossularia*)

If there's one crop a thief would be wise not to burgle it's got to be gooseberries. Not only is a lot of time spent on nicking gooseberries, which must increase your chance of getting caught, but also your DNA will almost certainly be left there as evidence in some shape or form. I often wonder what I would do if I ever caught someone robbing our plot. It might well involve part of a gooseberry bush. Our gooseberries, when they don't get pinched, are delicious. When I used to make wine, gooseberry was easily the most successful, tasting exactly how good champagne (vastly overrated in my book) should taste.
Variety: 'Invicta'.

Medlar (*Mespilus germanica*)

Our medlar has to be the most fiddled with tree on the plot. It was moved twice (the second time in a rather undignified, slapdash way) before it regained enough composure to allow fruit to form, but has now forgiven us and produces a glut of gloopy fruit for us to gorge on every year.

In France it is known as 'Cul de Chien', an unfortunate but quite accurate description. It is (until now) the only fruit that hasn't been nicked from our plot, which is odd as it stands right at the entrance and next to a footpath. The only reason that it is left alone is that would-be pilferers don't know what to do with it. The fruit is left to blet (rot)[1] before eating raw or made into purée or jam (see recipe on page 151). Spooned raw from its skin, the taste is not unlike dates and toffee with a touch of apple and cinnamon and, thankfully, not to everyone's taste.

Persimmon (*Diospyros kaki* 'Fuyu')

Persimmons are way short of the sort of nirvana you might associate with a mango, and to some they are an acquired taste, especially as, like medlars, they need bletting before they are edible. I tasted my first just a few years ago when Henry brought a sackful he'd been given by a friend in Hounslow. The persimmon, needing much warmth and sunlight to thrive and fruit, is a rare sight in the UK, so you can imagine my disappointment to hear that the tree was recently cut down by the owner.

On hearing the news I bought a tree of my own, but it spent a year in a pot before I found a suitable spot for it. I say suitable; the truth is that it was the only place where it could conceivably get enough sun to stand any chance of bearing fruit – smack bang in the middle of the plot. How it will fare, I've no idea. If it gets too big it may have to be pruned to stop it casting too much shade on other beds.

FROM TOP Gooseberry; Medlar; Persimmon.

Quince (*Cydonia oblonga*)

Quite why it has taken me so long to plant a quince tree is a constant source of bewilderment and annoyance. In the seventeenth century this was the daddy of

---

[1] Rot is quite a strong and misleading definition for 'blet'. Bletting is where the fruit decays internally to a point where the flesh is suitably soft and squidgy and the tastes amplified to perfection. Once they start fermenting the moment is lost.

Quince

the orchard with more recipes for this odd-looking fruit than for apples and pears. The slightly misshapen form of a quince always reminds me of the bony skull of a hare. The scented dog-rose-like flowers are delightful and the fruit itself is delicious baked in syrup or as a flavorsome 'hit' to lift an apple pie. Its popularity with the upper classes in the seventeenth century is largely down to its use as marmalade or paste. Known as quiddany or Genoa paste, the pectin-rich jelly could be used to mould decorative shapes and patterns and was therefore a versatile ingredient for confectionery. It was also used grated and infused in brandy to make a cordial known as Ratafia of Quinces.

Our Iranian quince, planted in February 2010, will probably take around five years to fruit. It will be suitably revered to the point of embarrassment when the first quince is picked, especially as some of my mother's ashes have been scattered at its feet.

Raspberry *(Rubus idaeus)*

Raspberries trump strawberries every time on our plot in terms of yield and they taste better too. We grow an autumn variety called 'Joan J' which crops reliably from August to early November, and sometimes even later, by which time we are usually sick of them. Autumn varieties just need chopping back hard each winter, while summer fruiting varieties need more time spent on them tying in stems that will bear fruit the following year. They are probably the most sensuous fruit when it comes to picking. The faint resistance and then release as the drupe comes away from its conical anchor is as satisfying as bindweed roots that are pulled from the ground without breaking.

Redcurrants *(Ribes rubrum)*

My great aunt Ivy used to make a fine redcurrant and raspberry pie and that's probably the only reason I grow them. I suspect people make jam, sorbets and crumbles with them, but redcurrants (or whitecurrants for that matter) are a bit too tart and don't carry the same fascination for me as blackcurrants.

Redcurrants

Strawberry *(Fragaria × ananassa)*

Some people are very organised with their strawberries, with rows of beefy plants cropping copiously each year. Ours have been a bit hit and miss, falling prey to slugs, mice, squirrels and birds when grown deliberately but producing the odd treat if left to run their own course in obscure and often shadier parts of the plot. They like fertile soil and probably need more compost and water than we tend to give them if they are to cope with our sandy soil.

Varieties: 'Perfection'; 'Royal Sovereign'.

Strawberry

CHAPTER SEVEN

Children

My paternal grandfather, Cyril Barton West, kept a tidy garden.[1] Neat edges to his lawn, proudly accentuated by annuals (probably red salvia or begonias) in lines, gave a clue to his Edwardian manner. So well organised was he that I don't recall him ever doing any gardening, so my garden memories with him are mostly about picking strawberries, raspberries and other soft fruit. My maternal grandmother's garden, by contrast, was an unkempt wilderness worn out by boys' games and general neglect, but a large apple tree and head-high brambles made it just as fascinating a space to forage for food.

Children love gardens. They're where they learn to connect with nature, the seasons, the elements.

Children love gardens. They're where they learn to connect with nature, the seasons, the elements. Most are completely at home in a garden without having to be 'taught' anything and food can take the whole experience to another level.

Since the Grow Your Own renaissance at the turn of the millennium, there has been a significant rise in the number of children at Bushy Park allotments with more families taking on plots. This adds another rich layer to allotment culture and potentially an important one if predictions for more localised food production are realised when low fuel stocks start affecting the way we live.

Children who take a little time out from the computer screen and engage in outdoor activity will discover all the excitement and fascination it has to offer and will arm themselves with respect and passion for the natural world. Unearthing new potatoes and getting them in the pot within minutes or throwing freshly picked sweetcorn like an American football to the catcher at the grill is not only fun, it proves just how tasty freshly picked food can be.

But it's not always that simple so be prepared for things not going to plan. Humaira, my assistant, has three boys and has made a valiant attempt to get them interested in growing food. There was a reasonable amount of success in terms of sowing, growing and harvesting, but the plan fell to pieces when no amount of bribery would tempt them to eat the end results, despite their great pride in their endeavours. Nor can one assume that the parents are interested. Reading about growing food might be very

All four of Christine's grandchildren (including Florence opposite) have grown up knowing our plot. While they have spent many happy days there, their contribution to weeding is a little wanting.

---

[1] I've always been a little sad that Barton, the paternal family name, was never handed down. Not only would having a double-barrelled name like a special agent have made me more popular at school, it might also have given me a better chance in competing for work against the likes of Tom Stuart-Smith, Chris Bradley-Hole, James Alexander-Sinclair, et al.

appealing, but the reality is that many people barely have the time or inclination to cook these days, let alone grow their own food. Engaging children is therefore just as much about engaging adults.

Christine's four grandchildren have grown up knowing our plot. Birthdays, family gatherings and Guy Fawkes Nights have been celebrated there with them. Arrangements to visit us invariably come with a request from the children to spend time at the plot. The twins, Otis and Finton, are now teenagers, so hanging around with adults on a veg patch is endangering their south-east London street-cred, but I did manage to get them to help me shift a lorry-load of horse manure when they came to help build the pizza oven. The prospect of lighting a fire inside the oven to dry it out was obviously my trump bargaining tool, but the notion that *'everyone has to shovel at least a tonne of poo in their life . . . so you may as well get it over with in one go'* appealed to their warped sense of humour.

While the allotment might not be the coolest place for Otis and Finton to hang out, Florence and Otto are still young enough to feel the magic of the place and are more frequent visitors. It has given them fun and their parents the confidence to turn their small garden at home completely over to vegetables so that growing food is now part of their daily life and not just a special event. Taking interest and pride in the food they grow bodes well for their future. With the shortage of allotments and a shortage of time to keep them productive, it was the only way they would get a chance to have a go themselves.

Bribing the twins, Otis and Finton, to shift a ton of poo, using the chance of setting fire to the earth oven as currency.

Florence and Otto in their veg patch at home.

6th November 2010
Finton, Otis, Florence and Otto have come to the
allotment for a belated Guy Fawkes Night. We've
celebrated it here for several years now with a bonfire and
a few fireworks so it's something of a tradition for them.
This time we fired up the earth oven and cooked potatoes,
sweet chestnuts, beans and veggie bangers. It made a
warming hearth and an excellent supper, but I think the
children would have preferred a regular bonfire that they
could get closer to and tinker with. Otis was very excited
at being allowed to light his first firework. As he lit the
touch paper, I couldn't resist shouting BANG!!!! in his
ear. He may never forgive me but the memory will almost
certainly stick with him for the rest of his life.

It's amazing how children tend to look guilty when you take their picture next to a bonfire.

Bushy Park allotments have proved a magical place for children, not only in terms of gardening and seeing things grow, but also as a place to play, the importance of which shouldn't be underestimated. Allotment by-laws, however, can be restrictive, so it's best to be considerate and not let children wander over other people's plots.

Play exercises the mind as much as the body, a notion championed by a number of organisations such as 'Going Wild' (www.goingwild.net) which teach families to reconnect with nature and seek adventure and learning in wild spaces. Play fires the imagination, builds confidence and self-esteem, helps children to judge risk and eventually, through the process of growing food and plants, learn something of our responsibility to the welfare of our locality and ultimately to the planet.

Sowing seeds and seeing their efforts bear fruit (or roots) is genuinely fascinating to children, so it's hardly surprising to see more of them tagging along with their parents, often for whole days at the plot. Sustaining interest for a full day may not always be as easy as it sounds and contingency plans are worth having to ensure survival at the plot (in terms of making the day a success). It boils down to four essentials: warmth, food, water and fire. Keeping children warm and well fed are the first two essentials while fire and water, depending on your plot's by-laws and situation, can be very useful when all enthusiasm for the great outdoors wanes faster than you'd bargained for.

The most interesting vegetable for children to grow has got to be sweetcorn. It's something they know not just from mealtimes but also from visits to the cinema and funfairs, so discovering that it is one of the easiest vegetables to grow is usually a revelation to them. Seeds sprout quickly and seedlings grown in pots are very forgiving to clumsy fingers while they are transplanted. Picking the cobs and peeling away the outer leaves heightens the sense of expectation and savouring their sweetness within minutes of being picked completes a sensuous and memorable experience. Peas, too,

are of great interest to children as they rarely come across anything but frozen peas in the shops. Actually, frozen peas aren't at all bad but let a child eat peas straight from the pod and I'll guarantee that you won't have any left in the basket to take home. Even sprouts can grab a child's imagination. This amazes me as I hated sprouts and anything remotely cabbagey as a child, but Otis and Finton ask for seconds when it comes to home-grown sprouts. Again, it's the freshness that makes all the difference, unless, of course, they are just plain weird.

As far as fruit is concerned, while children are naturally drawn to strawberries and raspberries, blackberries remain the firm favourite of most children visiting our plot during the summer holidays. I'm always threatening to grub out the thicket of brambles that survived our initial clearance as they take up a fair amount of space which could be used to keep chickens, but the pleasure (not to mention the black tongues) that children get out of it is worth all the scratches.

The star attraction now, though, is probably the earth oven, largely because it combines fire, warmth and food all in one.[2] I appreciate that not everyone has the space, time or inclination to make an earth oven but it certainly has taken cooking at the plot to a new level. Seeing pizza dressed with freshly harvested food and then eaten straight from the oven is a real treat for any children visiting the plot.

As our plot is quite generous it offers opportunities for children to play without disturbing anyone else when they get bored with veg. The wilderness area and stream at the back is a place where they can escape into their own world and has provided a relatively safe environment for them. Of course, there have been accidents. Wasp stings, bee stings, stinging nettle stings, not to mention scratches, scrapes and all the usual stuff, but occasionally something more dramatic. Feet have been cut from taking off wellies to paddle in the stream and an arm broken after Finton fell from a tree, narrowly missing being impaled on a metal spike that was minding its own business as a sculpture. A relic from the days when I worked with sculptor Johnny Woodford, the spike is now mildly miffed about losing its sculpture status and being reclassified as a lethal weapon. It will remain, for now at least, on its side and out of sight.

Given that Health and Safety record, I think Cleve West's Allotment Day for Kids is a non-starter.

---

[2] Cooking in an earth oven might sound romantic and most of the time, when we have the time, it is. But lighting and maintaining a fire is time-consuming so we only use it when we're at the plot for a full day. While it's fun cooking at the plot, sandwiches and other food prepared at home are always a good idea when children are involved to keep them going when their reserves run low.

CLOCKWISE FROM LEFT Florence sowing seeds in the potting shed; Otis removing the sand mould from the earth oven; Mandy (a fellow plot-holder) introducing Otto and Florence to her hens; Dhundi's son, East, enjoying our hammock; Otis on poo-duty.

CHAPTER EIGHT

Wildlife

While we might curse grazing rabbits, shredding pigeons and pesky squirrels, the wildlife is a large part of the fun we get from the plot so nothing is harmed deliberately. Of course our patience is tested, often beyond what most people would consider reasonable, but we won't starve if things get eaten and there's usually enough for all parties concerned (making 'Our Plot' an all-inclusive notion I suppose).

What is interesting is how some people are completely unaware of animals and insects and what goes on around them. Just being slightly more in tune with your surroundings, a parallel world can be observed where the name of the game is survival.

The easiest way to spot wildlife is to try and fine tune your senses, mostly sight and sound. Peripheral vision is the greatest asset, but you need to give it a chance to work properly by staying still for a while and staring into the mid-distance looking at nothing in particular. If anything moves within your range of vision, you will almost certainly pick it up and be able to shift your gaze and focus on whatever has caught your attention. Tea breaks are best for this; a few moments of quiet amplifies and accentuates everything that is happening around you.

A parallel world can be observed where the name of the game is survival.

If you can get over the idea that everything is conspiring against you and understand that creatures are just going about their daily affairs, you're less likely to give up. Remember, it's business, not personal.

Bats

Twilight at the plot has us either frantically gathering tools before darkness or, on a more organised summer evening, watching a silhouetted display of bats gorging on the insect life that hangs out under the trees at the back of the plot. A bat box has been positioned in a large ash behind the stream but we've never seen any evidence that it has been occupied.

Bees and wasps

At the time of writing, keeping our own bees is still just a notion but we are very pleased to see all manner of bees, wasps and hoverflies sharing our airspace. Wasps and bumblebees (*Bombus terrestris*) often make their home at our plot. Usually in an

7th August 2010
There's a bumblebees' nest under the potting shed, the entrance to the nest being underneath the threshold of the entrance. Very inconvenient really as we have to be careful not to disturb their journey in and out. They are harmless and won't attack even if we get in their way but leaving the door ajar confuses them. They seem drawn to a scent at the base of the door, so leaving it open diverts them away from the entrance hole and some end up inside the shed battling the cobwebs. Whether we're inside or out, we have to keep the door closed.

abandoned mousehole or among the various log piles. It's not always convenient, but it's a validation of our all-embracing attitude to insects.

Blackbirds

Blackbirds have a recognisable song but it can vary from year to year. This season we have one that every so often slips the first line of the TV classic *Upstairs Downstairs* into its repertoire. I try to get others to see if they can recognise it, but of course it doesn't sing to order and I'm invariably left with the distinct feeling that people think this may be the first sign of madness.

LEFT Meadow Brown butterfly.
ABOVE The cinnabar moth caterpillar feeding on ragwort.

Butterflies and moths

Most gardeners love seeing butterflies and moths yet, ironically, can't stand the thought of caterpillars on their plants and won't think twice about killing them. Of course, we don't want our brassicas devoured so any leaves with cabbage white eggs or caterpillars are removed and put on the compost heap, where they might still enjoy a meal without doing too much damage to our crop. We are not experts when it comes to lepidopterology so may well have more visitors than the regular cabbage white, painted lady, peacock, red admiral and tortoiseshell, all of which compete with hoverflies for nectar from the *Verbena bonariensis* that has seeded itself all over the plot. The cinnabar moth is also a frequent visitor, taking advantage of ragweed when it pops up, so we are careful not to disturb the tiger-striped caterpillars that feed on its foliage. The hummingbird hawkmoth (which once had me on the phone to the RSPB reporting a sighting of an actual hummingbird would you believe) has been seen just once so far, again beguiled by the verbena, a valuable food source for many insects.

Ducks

The stream and our small pond attract three ducks every spring, two shifty males and a nervous looking female. Frankly they look absurd, like adults in a child's paddling pool pretending that it's the most natural thing in the world. The female has a really tough time of it, flying around trying to get on with her day without the licentious and often violent behaviour of the males waiting to exert their dominance. I think the pond, being so small, is her sanctuary where there just isn't room enough for flappy-quacky-hanky-panky.

Foxes

A fox is always a welcome sight on our plot and they do reasonably well on a mixture of rodents, rabbits, birds and the scraps of food we put onto the compost heap.

Occasionally, while we're working for any length of time in the potting shed, a fox will pop over to the plot to see what's available. One once turned up with a squirrel in its mouth, which is good for us as squirrels do far more damage on our plot than foxes. Of course, they can ruin someone's day if they get into a chicken run but it amazes me how people get apoplectic about foxes killing their chickens when they themselves are guilty of leaving the coop open for the fox to get in. Foxes are famous for going a bit bonkers and killing every hen they see, often without eating them, but that's what they do. This should be more than enough reason to make sure that your hens are well protected.

One thing that fascinates me (and disgusts others) is a fox's inclination to leave its calling card on our table where odd crumbs are left for birds.

A fox having a nose just outside the potting shed.

Grass snakes and slow-worms

I was hoping that by the time I got to the end of this chapter I'd have seen my first grass snake at the plot. They are rare but have been spotted by two neighbouring plot-holders who share the stream at the back. The stream is a very useful conduit which keeps its activities private and offers a relatively safe environment in which to hunt and travel. A sighting by someone else, however, while I was writing this book brought to light just how dangerous it can be for these creatures when venturing onto the plot.

Part of the reason for moving my compost heaps to the back of the plot near to the stream was to increase my chances of spotting a grass snake as the warmth of a compost heap makes it an attractive nesting site. Even if they are there, it's no guarantee that we'll see one.

Slow-worms are shy creatures, too, so sightings are also rare. A sheet of corrugated metal laid where it catches the sun is a happy hiding place for a slow-worm, and I've put one out to atone for killing two the last time I used a strimmer. Nothing so far except for a fat toad and a few daft slugs that couldn't have picked a worse sleeping partner.

Herons

Another bird which gets pestered by the local jackdaw hoodies is the heron. Like prehistoric pterodactyls they screech to announce their displeasure at being heckled or moved on, but generally enjoy the space that Bushy Park has to offer and especially the Longford River where they spend much of the day feeding.

Jackdaws

Routines, customs and habits are always good to emphasise and cement a connection with the spirit of the place. While these might centre around human activity they are more often provided by nature. The seasons, the weather, plants and animal life provide much of it for us and one of the most powerful daily events is the sight and sound of jackdaws flocking back to their roost at dusk. Like the church bells in France at 6pm they tell you that it's time to pack up. Spending all of

9th June 2010
Rick found a snake today in his shed. The poor creature was tangled in plastic netting. Fortunately Henry was at hand and between them they were able to hold the creature steady enough to cut the netting and release it back into the stream. He thinks it was a grass snake as it had a yellow band around its neck. I tell him that you can tell the difference between a harmless grass snake and the poisonous adder by the eyes. A grass snake has round pupils whereas the adder has more menacing slits. We both agree that few people would consider getting that close to make a judgement.

10th April 2011
Yanked the tarpaulin from the compost today and was ecstatic to find a 60cm long grass snake. In the ensuing panic (the grass snake trying to find cover and me fumbling for my iPhone to get a picture of the frightened creature), I realised that even if I did get a shot (I didn't) there was little hope of it being use as, barring a few minor text chang the book had more or less been pu to bed. Oh well, the fact that I've seen one is satisfying enough.

their day foraging in Bushy Park, they gather in nearby trees within earshot of our plot, cackling and cavorting before one of them makes the move to go. Christine is besotted with them and always makes everyone stop to enjoy their majestic fly-by. It's an odd association but the sight and sound of jackdaws, wherever I am, will always remind me of her.

Kestrels

Anyone who has seen Ken Loach's film *Kes* will have a fondness for kestrels. Nesting in the trees just behind our plot, they feast all day on the abundance of rodents that are common to our plot and are troubled only by the jealous attentions of jackdaws and crows. Occasionally one will sup on a tree branch nearby.

The mouse and rabbit are bona fide allotment residents. The rat is a stunt rat from prop-makers, Keir Lusby, at Shepperton Studios.

Mice

Mice give us the run around in small doses and are therefore one of the easiest animals to live with. Their main objective is to get at your pea seeds or those that have just germinated and they do most damage when they manage to get into the greenhouse. Many people use traps, some bagging up to seven in a day, but a mouse caught by its snout is a sorry sight for us so we use humane traps and release them nearer the park boundary. Of course they come back. They know where their bread is buttered.

Rabbits

Finding a kit (a baby rabbit) at my feet in my potting shed under which rabbits have bred regularly for several years, I did the obvious thing. I took it by the neck and put it back at the entrance to its burrow. I can't kill a slug deliberately so how on earth can I wring the neck of a mammal? OK picking lettuce and leaving it at the burrow entrance may be going a little too far, and I think I have hardened my attitude of late to a point where if I caught one again I would have to put it on the other side of the boundary fence. No one would believe that I spent my teenage years in the country.

Rats

Few people would give rats the time of day but we have a quiet admiration for them. They are wise animals that have survived what the world has thrown at them since the dawn of mankind and we have seen them come and go at our plot, but they are never so much of a problem that we have to call in the council exterminator. They cause more problems for those who keep chickens as rats are attracted to the feed. Their smell is distinctive and not altogether pleasant but their ingenuity and instinct for survival are fascinating. That's not to say that we encourage them as rats carry Weil's disease.[1] Hygiene, therefore, is important when eating at the plot, especially when children come to visit.

[1] Weil's disease is often carried by rats. The disease can be transmitted by water that has been contaminated with rats' urine coming in contact with broken skin or the mucous membrane.

Ring-necked parakeets

With grating voices like the aliens in the film *Mars Attacks!*, the cacophony of the ring-necked parakeets that are now common to south-west London has long lost its initial charm. In Delhi they look and sound wonderful. In Bushy Park they are simply wrong and they go about their business as if they own the place. Experts are unsure whether their ever increasing population (a flock of over one hundred birds is a common sight these days) harms other species of bird, but plot-holders have watched parrots take over the habitat of woodpeckers and owls in the trees that separate the allotments from Bushy Park. A traditional dawn chorus is now a rare thing at the plot and the persistent squawking can turn even the most devoted twitcher potty. Emerging leaves on trees and fruit are their main diet so it has become even more imperative to protect crops from birds.

7th September 2008

My early arrival disturbed a flock of parrots on an apple tree near the car park. On closer inspection I was amazed to find that the birds had munched a classic apple core shape on every apple on the tree. A rare photo opportunity which would have won prizes for sure. Amazingly, it turned out to be a day when I didn't have a camera with me. When I returned with one the following day they had plundered it again and most of the apples were gone. I'm sure people think I'm making it up.

Robins

The best friend of any gardener is the robin. Ours sticks close (like the 'daemons' in Philip Pullman's *Northern Lights*), gratefully exploiting disturbed ground or debris, especially during the leaner months when the ground is frozen. They are no fools. Some get overconfident and follow you into a shed or the greenhouse where a sudden movement invariably makes them panic and embarrass themselves by flying into panes of glass and looking ridiculous, but they soon get over it. David, our coffee-detector, has got so intimate with his robin that it berates him if he's late at the plot and will hop inside his van or shed and demand food from his knee.

BELOW The woodcrete bird box has three entrances to give tits more of a chance against predators such as magpies and jays.
RIGHT Amphibians, such as this common newt, hibernate under logs, planks and other debris.

Thrushes

Evidence of a thrush at the plot is always a cause for celebration. Not that their dexterous shell bashing will make much difference to our snail population, but their decline in numbers, most probably due to the irresponsible use of slug pellets, is saddening as they are one of our most handsome birds. They also have one of the most beautiful songs – distinctive in that a thrush will repeat its tune two or three times as Robert Browning knew:

> . . . *he sings each song twice over,*
> *Lest you should think he never could recapture*
> *The first fine careless rapture!*

Tits

Two birdboxes put up to encourage tits to nest have been occupied every year since they were placed at the back of the plot close to the tree line. The boxes are made from a mixture of wood-shavings, clay and cement.[2] So successful were they that it took just ten seconds for the first bird to enter the birdbox after I had fixed it in position and taken the ladder away.

---

[2] Available from www.alanaecology.com.

CLOCKWISE FROM LEFT
The Green June beetle
feeding on a cardoon
flower is also partial to soft
fruit; solitary bee on *Allium
atropurpureum*; hoverfly
on a flowering lettuce; a
harlequin ladybird feasting
on a courgette; stag beetle
larva in a wood-pile; a
regular ladybird; an adult,
male stag beetle.

This toad chose to reside in our greenhouse for much of the summer and looked very well on it too.

A yearly clean out is advisable but make sure you do this on the ground and not while up a ladder. I once had the misfortune to be cleaning out a birdbox *in situ* when fleas inhabiting the box detected the warmth of my hand and came at me like the bullets from a tommy gun, denting both my forehead and my pride.

Toads

We encounter more toads than frogs at the plot. Over the years we have got to know their favourite haunts under planks of wood, paving slabs and the like, which is important as they are less likely to suffer damage from heavy-handed clearing of debris. The compost heap is another favourite haunt over winter so it can take some time, when spreading compost, checking for the slightest movement so as to minimise the chance of these creatures getting skewered or cut in two. Occasionally we'll find a whole family of toads residing alongside a generous supply of slugs. Breakfast in bed. Exactly how many slugs they eat of an evening is impossible to imagine but, however many it is, it's nowhere near enough. Be careful, when relocating a toad, to handle it gently and not be too disgusted when it wees on you. It's simply a defence mechanism.

Woodpeckers

The familiar sound of the green woodpecker drilling for insects is strangely comforting in its repetition and rhythm. Its laughing call, which some mistake for a kestrel, can be heard throughout the day as it bounces from tree to tree in search of grubs. I saw one once land on the timber boards of our raised beds and ravage an ants' nest before leaving two streaks of pink poo and flying off. It turned out to be the best wood stain on the market, being fresh as the day it was deposited when the timber boards finally rotted.

Wrens

Private, bad tempered and busy, wrens are some of the most creative birds when it comes to nest building, the most memorable being the one that made a nest in the pocket of my jacket. Their agitated song and calls of alarm pepper the day as they flit low to the ground foraging among brambles and the most inaccessible parts of the allotment. One of our smallest and most fascinating birds.

I'm sure the birds we see at our plot can find more than enough food to live on in and around the tree line behind our plot but we still put food out for them, especially when the weather makes life difficult for them in winter.

28th December 2010

A whole day spent at the plot to work off Yuletide excess. These few days before the New Year are the most precious in terms of being able to catch up on a whole host of tasks that need doing before spring. Christine is at home nursing bruises after slipping on the ice on Boxing Day so I work alone clearing paths, spreading compost, pruning espaliers. Few people here today and it's quiet except for bells from the local church which ring all afternoon and well into twilight. I stand by our quince tree to listen and watch silhouettes fade into the night when I notice a wren land close by before finding its way into a bird box on the Wonky Shed. It's the first time I have ever seen a bird using it. Seconds later, a second wren lands near the box and deftly slips inside. With the freezing temperatures we've had of late, it's heartening to know that these two are relying on a good old-fashioned snuggle to get through this tough winter.

21st November 2010

David reports that someone has seen a pike in the stream at the back of the plot. He's puzzled as to how the pike got there as the stream is so narrow in parts. I immediately know what it is. A couple of years ago someone on the plot was given a baby alligator gar (Atractosteus spatula), a primitive alligator-like fish full of teeth from North America that can grow 10 feet long and weigh 90kg. It was kept in a fish tank in a shed for a while but then (rather irresponsibly) released into the stream 'to give it a better life'! I'm amazed that it survived the freezing temperatures of last winter and wonder about its chances for the future. We really ought to try and catch it and find an aquarium to give it a better chance of survival but, until then, stories of the toothy creature that lurks in the stream at the back of the plot waiting for anything to fall in is proving very popular with the children.

CHAPTER NINE

Problems

I began writing this book determined to give an honest account of our allotment experience so that anyone considering a slice of The Good Life could get a reasonable idea of what they were letting themselves in for. It should be clear by now that an allotment is a commitment and one that needs a little thought before taking it on, especially when they are so scarce.

For us it provides not only a much larger space in which to grow food but also an escape. Being there feels a million miles from city life. We are lucky. Not every allotment is blessed with a view to the nether regions of a Royal Park where deer and other wildlife roam freely. If I could only have a much smaller patch with a view of surrounding houses, I'm not sure that I'd want one, but of course it's all relative to what you know and what's available. People tend to make the best of what they've been given. There are both advantages and disadvantages and a love–hate relationship often develops, time being a major factor in both cases. I don't want to make this sound too gloomy, because it really is far from that, but some newcomers last less than a year so it's worth just touching on the negatives to give a more balanced perspective.

Late night slug patrols at the plot are essential after early summer showers, so it's very dispiriting to hear rain falling just as you're about to go to bed.

Hand on heart, I would happily swap the allotment for a larger garden where our no-kill policy would be a more realistic and effective method of husbandry. Crops are so much easier to police when they're on your doorstep. Late night slug patrols at the plot are essential after early summer showers, so it's very dispiriting to hear rain falling just as you're about to go to bed. A bigger garden would also allow us more scope for ornamental planting although, as a garden designer, making gardens for other people is usually enough to satisfy such creative urges.

While the 'camping' or 'decamping' aspect of the allotment appeals to my bushcraft instincts, far too much time is taken up with ferrying stuff to and fro, to the point where we are in a constant state of flux. Cooking at the allotment involves even more forward planning and can be a palaver, especially

when we are using the earth oven, which can take a good three hours to fire up. Many of these 'negatives' are obviously time-related and can be made less frustrating by being organised but, occasionally, there are other factors that can make gardening away from home even more testing and, at times, quite dispiriting.

Vandalism

Wanton vandalism by outsiders is not uncommon on allotments, especially on urban plots. I have a feeling, however, that modern technology has actually helped to reduce the incidence of vandalism in recent years by keeping would-be perpetrators indoors at a computer or transfixed by a games console. Also, the popularity of growing food means that there is much more activity at allotments than there ever has been, especially during late evenings (when vandalism usually occurs) as plot-holders squeeze in whatever hours they can around a busy lifestyle.

Ten years ago I remember several incidents of broken greenhouses and damaged sheds. It happened in waves and was very difficult to predict. Such pointless antisocial behaviour, however petty, is completely alien to the harmony that usually exists at allotments and is therefore accentuated to the point of outrage. Damage to greenhouses probably causes most distress as they are extremely costly and time-consuming to construct or repair. Invariably it comes down to security, so locked gates have been the norm at our allotment for some years now. We also have a good relationship with the local police, who take the issue of vandalism seriously.

Theft and intimidation

Theft happens to a greater or lesser degree on most allotments and Bushy Park allotments are no exception. The intensity and regularity of incidents fluctuates from season to season and, while perpetrators occasionally come from outside, more often than not it will be a fellow plot-holder or one of their guests who is to blame.

People are often surprised to hear this, assuming that there is a mutual code whereby allotment holders respect each other's property and produce. Most do, but it only takes a few to tarnish any notion of the good life. It's not as if it's something new either. Several people I've spoken to remember pilfering during the Dig for Victory campaign of the Second World War, particularly when air-raids forced people into underground shelters, providing a clear opportunity for others to steal from gardens and allotments. It's hard to imagine but those were dark days and hard times. There's no real reason for stealing today.

Catching thieves red-handed is almost impossible. Man-traps (Heath Robinson contraptions involving either a bucket of paint or a vat of liquid manure) have been considered but quickly dismissed, as we would almost certainly end up being the victims. Photographic or video evidence is the only thing that will prove anything and with digital cameras, heightened awareness and good timing we may, one day, get lucky.

It's hardly surprising that stealing occurs at allotments. Most people are guilty of scrumping at some time or other during childhood, so it follows that outsiders coming into an allotment might see no harm in picking a few strawberries close to a footpath. It's bad enough losing crops to the wildlife let alone people, so allotment folk are inclined to go apoplectic when they find their plot plundered.

A bare fruit tree might seem a trivial thing compared with what you hear on the news every evening, and of course it is. But given the amount of time, energy and emotion that people put into growing their food, it's understandable that most victims would find at least 50 things to do with a pitchfork if they ever got their hands on the culprit.

Soft fruit is probably the most popular choice of thieves as it is expensive to buy. Birds and squirrels obviously like a bit of fruit too when it's available, but they tend to help themselves during daylight hours. They also leave traces of their activities and, contrary to popular belief, don't strip a whole bush bare in just a few hours. So if you arrive at your plot one morning to find your bushes robbed completely, you can be fairly certain that someone has been keeping a close eye on your plot's progress and chosen the right moment for their raid. Occasionally we get reports of several plots being ransacked for one specific crop, which suggests that the stolen crops are being sold.

Blackberries are commonly cultivated at allotments but their ubiquity on overgrown allotments makes people assume that they can help themselves as if they are doing the allotment holder a favour. In the past, some people have got so fed up with repeated pilfering that they have resorted to putting signs up saying that the whole crop has been sprayed with an insecticide and is unsuitable for human consumption. The fruit was still taken, the robbers being either unconcerned about their health (or the health of those to whom they were going to sell the blackberries) or illiterate.

Bitter melon is hardly the most attractive name for a vegetable but it's actually a very healthy option being packed with vitamins.

Our Vietnamese friends, Chi and his family, rarely have anything stolen from their plot largely because robbers don't know what to do with bitter melon and some of the more exotic vegetables they grow. We usually get something taken each year. Gooseberries seem to be the favourite booty; pears, too, particularly Josephine de Malines, a late variety and therefore a beacon of temptation when there is little else on offer.

Even more unsettling was a period when people were being intimidated by unsociable behaviour. It's not something I really wanted to cover in this book, but there were several years when elderly and vulnerable individuals were intimidated enough to give up their plots. It soon became evident that families and close-knit groups of friends were conspiring to take over as many plots as possible and sub-letting plots to strengthen a sort of gang-farming culture.

Trying to prove this was almost impossible and there were times when the council had their work cut out trying to remove some of the worst offenders, but eventually they did and things have returned to normal.

It's easy for such stories to become so inflated as to put people off, but the positives really do outweigh the negatives.

Bushy Park has the biggest allotment site in the borough so open days are useful events where people can get to know each other and share information, experiences and problems.

In the ten years we have been at Bushy Park allotments things are generally better when there is a proactive committee which encourages people to get involved, even if it's just baking a cake for the open day.[1] This means that when there is occasional pilfering there is support and encouragement from those with their ear to the ground. In any case, the amount of food that is bartered and given away shows that the vast majority of allotment folk are happy to share the fruits of their labour. This is possibly one of the most life-affirming aspects of allotment culture which, for many, plays such an important role in their way of life.

[1] At the time of writing we are fortunate to have Phil Iddison as our chairman. His level head, dynamic approach and expertise in growing superb vegetables has already had a marked effect on the morale at Bushy Park allotments. Apart from anything else, I suspect this will mean more cake for open days.

CHAPTER TEN

Food and recipes

Eating al fresco always feels a bit of a bonus in the UK, where the weather is just a little less reliable than, say, Provence. Our first lunches at the plot were sandwiches, either made at home or bought en route, and this is still the preferred choice when we're working and time is short. A flask of coffee, too, was an essential motivator and, of course, a generous assortment of biscuits.

With time always in short supply it's easy to forget about one's stomach and to go on working through elevenses, lunch and tea. It's not a healthy way to garden and there have been many occasions when we have returned home exhausted and parched like John Mills et al. in the final scene of the film *Ice-Cold in Alex*, though considerably more grumpy. In truth this would probably happen every time if I was on my own, but Christine is far more practical and always keen to keep the monster at bay with frequent snacks and coffee breaks.

Increasingly we adopted a leisurely approach to lunch, supper and family picnics

Things changed a little when I built a table from a large slab of oak left over from a show garden at the Chelsea Flower Show.[1] Positioned under a self-seeded oak at the back of the plot, the table immediately suggested a more salubrious way of dining. It's like the kitchen table at home,[2] a natural draw to anyone visiting, and it sets the scene for a more social part of the plot, where shade from trees makes it a difficult place to grow food. Quick, working lunches were still par for the course but at least we now had somewhere comfortable to sit.

On buying a small gas stove, however, we were suddenly equipped to become a little more adventurous and increasingly we adopted a leisurely approach to lunch, supper and family picnics. It also meant that Christine, a barista at heart, could make fresh coffee in a percolator or cafetière. Offer her instant and she's quite likely to faint on the spot or, at the very least, look at you as though you've suggested drinking a cup of liquid manure. On organised days we'll grind coffee at home but a hand-operated coffee mill is stored in one of the sheds just in case we forget. David, who will travel some distance for a decent cup

We've come a long way since the early days of hastily prepared packed lunches and snacks on-the-hoof. Occasionally, when we're not cooking and eating, we grow veg.

[1] This 1.8m × 1m slab of oak was surplus to requirements for the Merrill Lynch Garden in 2001. Johnny Woodford helped me load in into a van but every time I turned up with it at the allotment there was no one there to help unload it. Eventually, by using logs and a little Roman ingenuity, I managed to roll the slab 30m to where it still sits under an oak at the back of the plot. It took two hours, after which people came out of hiding.

[2] For some reason, as if to scupper our plans for a more sophisticated touch, it has served as the perfect spot for the local fox to take an elevated crap, which is why Christine is fastidious about using a tablecloth whenever we eat.

of coffee, has an uncanny knack of turning up just when the coffee is brewed, even with an east wind blowing, so, as a matter of course, we put out three cups and saucers. There is enormous temptation to let coffee waft in his general direction and then hide when he eventually wanders over, but Christine says it's not only childish but cruel to play such tricks.

With a greenhouse there is even scope for eating at the plot during winter. Just a little sunlight is enough to make it cosy enough and, even with a howling gale outside, lunch in what feels like the conservatory is really quite a treat. The danger of improved catering facilities was obvious and very soon we were wrestling with our consciences watching bindweed emerge while tucking into another bowl of nettle soup (see page 150) or hot crumpets, coffee and blackcurrant jam (see page 153).

The simple act of roasting chestnuts over the embers of a bonfire on a cold day is both physically and mentally warming.

Bonfires at the plot are an indulgence on our part and serve not just for winter tidy-ups but also as a surrogate for the open fire we don't have at home. Apart from being generally out of step with environmental awareness, they can be antisocial and are therefore banned during the summer months, but when we do have one it's impossible to resist boiling a kettle, baking potatoes or warming soup. Chestnuts are a real treat to accentuate and celebrate the festive season and, when we're really organised, an open fire is the best place to deep fry onion bhajees as it saves stinking the kitchen out at home. With that in mind we are always on the lookout for useful tools and campfire gadgets. The best to date is a simple piece of ironwork bought in Normandy that can be pushed into an open fire to make an instant shelf on which to stand a kettle or a pot of soup. Old pots and cauldrons have taken on a second life and our kitchen at home is starting to look neglected by comparison.

Christopher Woodward and members of the Garden Museum no doubt thinking to themselves, 'I can't believe he's just served us soggy bhajees!'

15th August 2009

Members of the Garden Museum arrive to spend some time at the plot. Christopher Woodward, the director, has injected a huge amount of energy into the museum and turned it into a hive of activity, and it is now a dynamic place where many in horticulture can meet on a regular basis rather than relying on flower shows as places to bump into colleagues and friends. We show them around our plot and Henry allows them to pick some of his plums before I heat up the kuri for onion bhajees. While everyone was complimentary about the bhajees, I noticed, a bit too late really, that they were a little undercooked and it irked me for the rest of the day. There's nothing worse than a soggy bhajee. Have made a note to invite them back some day so that I can atone for this faux pas.

With such means of cooking at our disposal, the allotment suddenly became a more attractive place for family and friends to visit. This is more important than I first realised and now, while growing food is still the main attraction, cooking at the plot has become such an essential part of our life there that we rarely entertain at home. One large family gathering a year is held at the plot while other, smaller and more spontaneous occasions occur whenever we can fit them in and are largely guided by the weather.

With no electricity and no hot water on tap, preparing feasts and banquets away from home is more laborious. It's the equivalent of camping. Much time is spent preparing and clearing away but that's become an acceptable part of the deal. Food prepared at home can make things easier but seasonal veg, especially salads and new potatoes, make all the difference when they are prepared within minutes of harvesting.

Earth oven

Without doubt, the most exciting project we've ever undertaken at the plot has been building an earth oven. On the face of it, it has nothing to do with growing food but increasingly over the years we have taken to spending whole days at the plot and cooking proper meals there. At home, bread-making has become part of our weekly routine, so it made sense to combine the two.

The idea came when new water mains were laid in the winter of 2008–9. Despite the luxury of having water on tap reasonably close to our plots, a few plot-holders were more than a little grumpy when clay from trenches (dug in atrocious weather) turned paths into quagmires.

Sainsbury's John, positive as ever, saw this as an opportunity and made a prototype oven by moulding clay around bags of gravel. We tested it by baking bread and pizza to celebrate his birthday and I knew instantly that I had to build one of my own. Soon a large bag of puddling clay, left over from a pond project, found its way to the plot. There it sat for months while I thought about the best way of siting and building the oven. There was always the temptation to build it quickly but I wanted to make something that would last. Eventually I found the book *Build Your Own Earth Oven* by Kiko Denzer and spent a month or so absorbing it before making a start in the late winter of 2009.

Bricks and hardcore at the plot were used to make the base. The clay, mixed with sharp sand, did for the first layer of the dome and subsoil from the site itself was dug for the insulation layers. The process tickled my primitive synapses; it was completely absorbing and satisfying. Having my mother help mix and make the first layer of clay has elevated its importance, and it now stands not just as a hearth to draw people but also as a memorial to her and a symbol of honest hard work and her dedication to helping others.

The only reservations I have are the amount of wood needed to fuel it and the fact that it distracts us from some of the more important tasks at the plot.

8th July 2010

Arrive at 4pm to fire up the earth oven. Have promised pizza for some very tired people working at the Hampton Court Flower Show. I use charcoal this time to reduce the amount of smoke and speed things up a bit but it still takes over two hours for the oven to reach the right temperature. Pizza toppings are prepared at home this time, which helps to make things easier, but it still feels like a major undertaking. The quality of pizza, though, makes it all worthwhile. Joe Swift, Jekka McVicar and people from the RHS and BBC drift in. Sainsbury's John, who's meant to come and officially open the oven, is laid low with a migraine, which is a shame as the pizza party is a great success and continues well after dark.

Recipes from the allotment

I thought I'd include a few of our favourite recipes. Some are from my family, others are from fellow allotment holders and a few have been snaffled from well-thumbed cookery books in our kitchen.

1. Onion bhajees
2. Putchani
3. Aloo baigan (potato and aubergine)
4. Squash risotto
5. Parsnip soup with medlar jam
6. Pasta fagioli
7. Blackened aubergine chutney
8. Zucchini all'uovo
9. Nettle soup
10. Vietnamese cabbage salad
11. Medlar jam
12. Courgette ratte
13. Pizza
14. Blackcurrant jam
15. Beetroot and French bean salad
16. Baked blackberry and stem ginger pudding
17. Carrots braised with cumin, saffron and garlic
18. Cavolo Nero with garlic and Parmesan
19. Broad bean pilaf with raisins and almonds
20. Boston baked beans
21. Baked pears with honey, marsala and bay

1. Onion bhajees

My grandmother, Vida St Romaine, played Ava Gardner's mother in the film *Bhowani Junction*. My mother and other members of the family also had parts in the film as extras and it is highly likely that these bhajees were eaten on the set for lunch. As this is simply the best bhajee recipe on the planet, Ava Gardner would have found them irresistible. It's a forgiving recipe in terms of quantities (I had to make a special batch to work out quantities as it's usually done by feel), but it takes a bit of practice to get the batter to the right consistency and the oil hot enough so the bhajees are neither over- nor undercooked.

Makes about 12–16 bhajees

4 medium sized onions, thinly sliced
350 g gram flour (chickpea flour)
2 tsp turmeric
250 ml water
pinch of baking powder
salt and pepper
4–6 cloves garlic
2.5 cm nub of ginger
some chopped chillies to taste
handful of chopped fresh coriander including stems
lemon juice
sunflower or corn oil for deep-frying

Sift gram flour, turmeric and baking powder into a large mixing bowl. Add garlic, ginger, chillies, salt and pepper and mix well. Add water little by little, stirring all the time and making sure all the gram flour is mixed without lumps. The final batter should have a consistency between pancake and cake mix. Err on the side of too thick rather than too thin. Stir in chopped coriander and squeeze in a little lemon juice. Heat corn or sunflower oil in a wok or a karahi over a hot stove. Oil is ready when a small drop of batter sinks to the bottom then rises after a few seconds.

At the last minute add the sliced onions to the batter and begin frying. Work quickly as the onions will release their liquid into the mix and will eventually make it too runny. Place several spoonfuls of the mix into the hot oil and let them sizzle for three minutes or until golden brown. Remove from oil with a slotted spoon and let them drain on a plate with kitchen paper. These are best eaten warm but can be eaten cold if necessary. They are best reheated in an oven (not microwave) where they can retain an element of crispness.

Variations of this mix can be made using other vegetables such as beans, courgettes, courgette flowers and aubergines.

2. Putchani

Our family's spicy tomato relish recipe which was a very popular Anglo-Indian side dish. The special ingredient here is panch puran, the Bengali five spice mixture of cumin, fennel, nigella, mustard and fenugreek seeds.

4 large onions, diced	2 tbsp tomato purée
4–6 tbsp mustard oil	juice of 1 lemon
6 tbsp panch puran	1 tbsp vinegar
2 kg ripe tomatoes	jaggery (unrefined sugar)
3 cm cube of ginger	or honey
6 cloves garlic	salt and pepper
fresh chillies to taste	a cup of water

In a large, heavy pot fry onions in the mustard oil (this helps preserve the relish).

When translucent add panch puran and cook for a minute until the seeds pop. Add ginger, garlic and chillies and cook for a few more minutes until the aromas are released. Stir in the tomato purée, lemon juice, vinegar, salt and pepper and the honey or jaggery. Add just enough of the water to keep ingredients from sticking. When you have a smooth paste add the chopped tomatoes, the rest of the water and stir thoroughly. Boil down so that there is no liquid left – this is important; otherwise the chutney will not keep. When the mixture is cool pour into sterilised jars and seal.

3. Aloo baigan (aubergine and potatoes laced with fenugreek)

This recipe is so simple, so quick and so delicious that I'm constantly amazed every time I cook it. The subtlety of flavour comes from fenugreek seeds used at the start and amchoor (mango) powder used at the end. It's from Julie Sahni's *Classic Indian Vegetarian and Grain Cooking* (William Morrow), one of the few cookery books that reflects the real taste of the Indian cuisine.

Serves 4
500 g aubergine
500 g potatoes (a waxy variety that holds its shape like 'Charlotte' or 'Ratte')
¾ tsp turmeric
1½ tbsp ground coriander
½–1 tsp cayenne pepper
1½ tsp salt
4 tbsp light vegetable oil
¾ tsp fenugreek seed
1 tsp mango powder (amchoor)

Cut the aubergine, unpeeled into 2.5cm pieces or cubes. Peel the potatoes and cut them into 2.5cm cubes. Put the vegetables in a bowl. Sprinkle on the turmeric, ground coriander, cayenne and salt and mix well to coat evenly with the spices.

Heat the oil in a large skillet over high heat for three minutes. Add the fenugreek seeds and fry until they turn dark brown (10–15 seconds). Add the vegetables, shake the pan a few times, and let the vegetables sizzle undisturbed for one or two minutes. Fry the vegetables, turning them, for five minutes or until the spices start clinging to the vegetables and the aubergine looks limp and begins to steam. Lower the heat and cook, covered, for 20 minutes, turning the vegetables often to ensure that they are cooking evenly. Be careful not to break the fragile pieces of vegetables. Sprinkle on the mango powder and fry uncovered, turning them regularly, for five minutes or until they look glazed. Serve warm or at room temperature.

4. Squash risotto

This is a version of Nadine Abensur's pumpkin and parsley risotto with white wine in *The Cranks Bible*. It's one of those recipes that you'll find in many cookery books but Ms Abensur's description of the art of risotto making, likening the process to a dance, encourages you to feel your way and trust your instincts. You really need a squash or pumpkin that will hold its shape and have enough 'meat' to hold its own throughout the process and taste good, so stick to butternut squash or the bright orange Uchiki Kuri. Like many risottos, it's rich and filling.

Serves 2–4

1 medium to large butternut squash
salt and black pepper
1 bunch oregano, chopped
2 tbsp olive oil
½ litre Marigold vegetable bouillon stock
50 g butter
1 red onion, finely chopped
6 cloves garlic, whole
2 cloves garlic, finely chopped
½ to 1 glass white wine
150 g arborio rice
50 g Parmesan cheese, finely grated
small handful of chopped parsley to garnish

Preheat oven to 200°C/400°F/gas mark 6. Cut the squash into quarters and remove the seeds. Chop into 5cm pieces and put into a roasting pan with whole cloves of garlic. Season with pepper, salt and oregano, then drizzle with olive oil. Roast for 30 minutes or until the flesh is soft and the skin has shrivelled. Squeeze out garlic cloves from their skins and leave to cool. Bring the stock to the boil and simmer.

Melt 25g of the butter in a large frying pan over a medium heat and fry the onion and chopped garlic until soft. Add the rice and fry and stir for a couple of minutes to coat the grains. Return to the heat and slowly add ladles of stock while stirring. Adjust the heat up or down to keep control of this process. The rice shouldn't be so dry as to stick to the pan; neither should it be swimming in stock liquid. Keep adding stock and stir until the rice has absorbed nearly all the liquid.

Add the chunks of cooked squash and whole garlic. Add the wine, remaining butter and Parmesan and stir briefly. Serve garnished with parsley.

5. Parsnip soup with medlar jam

I'm writing this recipe feeling very resentful, having just dug up all my parsnips (in the spirit of experimental planting for the *Daily Telegraph* garden at Chelsea) to be potted up for the Chelsea Flower Show. To make matters worse, a small, misshapen runt of a parsnip that somehow found its way back home was absolutely delicious when roasted, and I'm now questioning the sacrifice we've made in the name of nothing more than novelty. If we don't win a Gold Medal for having had to forfeit parsnips at Christmas, I will be more than a little disgruntled. Occasionally, to inject even more nuttiness to this recipe, we roast the parsnips before cooking them but this is quick and easy.

Serves 4
2 tbsp olive oil
1 onion, chopped
1 clove garlic, crushed
1 carrot
450 g parsnips
5 cm nub of fresh root ginger chopped
1 litre Marigold vegetable bouillon stock
salt and freshly ground black pepper
medlar jam and/or crème fraiche to garnish

Heat the oil, add the onion and sauté gently till translucent. Add the garlic and ginger and fry for a few seconds before adding the carrot and parsnips. Stir the ingredients and cook for a further five minutes.

Add the stock, bring to the boil and then simmer for 30 minutes or until the vegetables are tender.

Allow to cool, taste for seasoning, then purée in a food processor or blender. Add a little extra stock if the soup is too thick.

Reheat gently before serving with either crème fraiche and/or a dollop of medlar jam (see page 151) as a garnish.

6. Pasta fagioli

A winter staple from Giuseppe which is both delightfully simple and wholesome. You can make this as spicy as your taste buds allow by varying the amount of chilli and pepper.

Serves 4
250g dry borlotti beans
1 clove garlic, finely sliced
pinch of dried chilli
1 stalk celery, finely chopped
1–2 tbsp tomato paste or 1–2 fresh tomatoes, chopped
2 tbsp olive oil
Salt and pepper to taste
400g pasta (you can use different types of pasta together)

If the beans are dry leave overnight to soak in cool water. Once soaked, place in a pan with the water and boil for 1 hour to soften. Check every once in a while to see that the pan still has water.

Once the beans are cooked (or, if using a tin, open and heat up the beans in their water) add the garlic, dried chilli, chopped celery, tomatoes or tomato paste, salt and pepper and olive oil. Tip the pasta into the same pot and cook according to the packet.

After about 10–15 minutes you should have a lovely, creamy, saucy pasta, which should be served with a great hunk of rustic bread.

7. Blackened aubergine chutney

Dhundi Raj Bhusal showed me this simple, tasty relish while we were having a barbeque at the plot. Use it to accompany any curry or mop a bowl of it up with naan bread for lunch.

Serves 2–4
1 medium aubergine
handful of green tomatoes
some chopped fresh chilli (¼–½ tsp)
1 clove garlic
small bunch of coriander
salt and pepper to taste
a good squeeze of lemon juice

Put the aubergine and the green tomatoes on the barbeque or open fire and char them until they are all black and squidgy inside. Then cut along the middle and scoop out the contents of both aubergines and tomatoes and mash.

Add the rest of the ingredients, mix and eat! It doesn't get simpler than that.

8. Zucchini all'uovo

In summer, when there is a glut of eggs from his chickens, Giuseppe cooks this on a gas stove at the plot for brunch. Sometimes he cooks more than he can handle and is more than generous to anyone who has the good fortune to be working nearby. As ever, cooking outside with the fresh ingredients, spontaneous meals like these are extra delicious and always memorable.

Serves 4
4 courgettes, cut into small cubes
1 onion, chopped
2 tbsp olive oil
100 g Parmesan cheese, grated
6 eggs
salt and pepper to taste

Fry the onion and courgettes in a frying pan with the olive oil. While these are softening and turning golden brown, beat the eggs, Parmesan and salt and pepper together.

Once the courgettes and onions are tender, add the egg mixture to the pan and mix to make a scrambled egg consistency.

Should either be served simply with bread or to accompany a main meal.

9. Nettle soup

We know summer has arrived when Christine dons rubber gloves to pick a bag of fresh stinging nettles from the plot to make this, one of our favourite soups.

Serves 6

225 g young nettle shoots (about 10 handfuls)
100 g butter
450 g onions, sliced
6 cloves garlic, sliced
1½ litres Marigold vegetable bouillon stock
150 g crème fraiche
sea salt and pepper to taste

Wash the nettle shoots, then melt the butter in a large saucepan and fry the onions gently over a low heat for 10 minutes until they are tender and translucent.

Add the garlic and cook gently for another 2 minutes. Add the nettles and stock and then bring to the boil. Once boiling, bring the heat down to a simmer for another 5 minutes.

Now liquidise to a smooth luscious green purée. It should remind you of freshly mown grass. Season generously and serve with a big dollop of crème fraiche in each bowl. Yum.

10. Vietnamese cabbage salad

Our Vietnamese friends, Chi, Thimy and their family, occasionally show up at open days with this simple but punchy salad.

Serves 4

200 g Vietnamese cabbage, finely sliced (Vietnamese cabbage is sweeter than the English varieties but not essential)
50 g carrot, coarsely grated
Vietnamese herbs to taste, roughly chopped (sweet basil, peppermint, spearmint, Vietnamese mint, perilla – there is no restriction on which types of herbs to use)
toasted peanuts, crushed

For the fish sauce dressing:
3 tbsp fish sauce
3 tbsp lime juice
2 tbsp sugar
1–2 chillies, finely chopped
1–2 cloves garlic, finely chopped

Mix the ingredients with fish sauce dressing and sprinkle with toasted peanuts.

11. Medlar jam

Mark Diacono gave me this recipe and, while it might seem a little fiddly, it's more forgiving than medlar jelly, which involves all that extra straining malarkey. In any case there's something more honest about medlar jam, which is more akin to the natural toffee-like gooeyness. Plop a teaspoon or two in a bowl of parsnip soup (see page 146). It's a marriage made in heaven.

Halve or quarter the medlars depending on size, put them in a pan and cover with water. Throw in a stick of vanilla (a whole one for a kilo), and simmer until the medlars turn pretty much to pulp.

Take out the vanilla pod. Sieve the pulp to extract the medlar seeds and any leathery bits – you might want to use your fingers a bit to get the worst of the seeds out while you're pressing the pulp through.

Weigh the pulp and add 70 per cent of the pulp's weight in sugar plus the vanilla pod split along its length – you want the tiny seeds to escape into the jam. Warm through slowly until the sugar has dissolved, then up the heat until it starts bubbling lightly. You may not have to cook it too long before you get to the point where the jam doesn't close round it immediately when you scrape a wooden spoon along the bottom of the pan. When that occurs, get it into sterilised jars. If you want to be more accurate about the setting point, drop a blob onto a cold saucer and leave it for a minute – if the jam sort of crinkles up when you push it on the plate, it's ready.

It's such a tasty jam – a cross between apples, figs and dates.

12. Courgette ratte

This is our staple for summer and one we rarely get bored with. It's quick to prepare and delicious, especially when the courgettes and tomatoes are fresh, so it's a dish we fall back on when we come home with little time to cook supper. Yellow courgettes (we grow 'Jemmer' and 'Parador' but it would be nice to find one that wasn't an F1 variety) have a sweeter taste than most green varieties and the colour makes for an especially attractive meal.

Serves 2
4–6 cloves garlic, sliced (more if you're a garlic nut like us)
4 tbsp olive oil (or, like us, a bit more if you like)
4–6 medium sized courgettes, halved and then sliced lengthways into ½ cm strips
handful of cherry tomatoes
handful of basil leaves
salt and pepper to taste

Heat the oil in a large saucepan or frying pan. Add the garlic to the oil and stir for a few seconds before adding the sliced courgettes. Season with a little salt and pepper. Fry on a medium heat (don't allow the garlic to burn, otherwise it will impart a slightly bitter taste) for about 20 minutes or until the courgettes start to brown. Lightly crush the cherry tomatoes, add to the courgettes and cook for a further 5 minutes so that any water from the tomatoes is reduced to whatever oil is left. Remove from heat, add torn basil leaves, cover pan and leave for another 5 minutes before serving. We like to serve ours on thick, buttered (yes!) slices of homemade bread that sponges up the delicious oil.

13. Pizza

Making pizza is easy and is less trouble than most people realise. The tricky bit is getting your oven to a high enough temperature in order to cook the dough quickly enough. Pizza cooked in our oven at home takes a good 13 minutes and often has a doughy texture to it. In our earth oven it will cook in three minutes and have a wonderful contrast of slightly burnt crispy bits and softer parts that make good pizza so moreish.

We make the dough at home and freeze it so that there's always some to hand if we make a spur of the moment decision to fire the oven up. This works well for us as the dough, once defrosted, is generally easier to shape than freshly made dough.

For 4–5 pizza bases

6 tsp dried yeast or three 7g sachets of quick yeast
30 g sugar
630 ml tepid water (40 46°C/105 115°F)
1 kg strong bread flour
1 tbsp olive oil
3 tspn (18 g) salt

Dissolve the sugar in half of the water. Sprinkle in yeast and stir.

Mix flour and salt in a large bowl. Make a well in the centre and add yeast mixture when it begins to froth.

Add remaining water, roughly mix for a few seconds with a spoon and then add the olive oil.

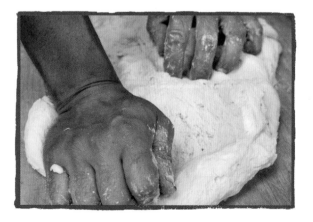

Bring the mixture together until it forms a ball, then knead for 5 or 10 minutes on a flat surface. If too dry, add a little more water. If too sticky, dust in a little extra flour. Aim for a silky texture that's not too difficult to push about.

Mould the dough into a ball and leave in a deep bowl covered with a damp cloth. In the right conditions (warm and draught-free) the dough should double in size within an hour. This might take longer in colder conditions.

The dough is now ready to be used for pizza so heat the oven to 240°C/475°F/gas mark 9. Divide the dough into 4 or 5 balls and roll out into a plate shape around ½–1 cm thick. Don't worry about getting it perfectly circular. The beauty of home-made pizza is that it should be slightly irregular in shape to give it more character and contrast in terms of texture.

A home-made tomato sauce as a base topped with a little of what you fancy and a scattering of cheese should be enough but don't overdo it. Too many toppings can kill a pizza and make it too wet to cook properly. Our favourite combo is tomato sauce, mushroom (pre-cooked in butter), garlic, sliced fresh tomato topped with mozzarella and garnished with a little basil, salt and pepper.

Put the pizza on a non-stick tray and bake for 5–10 minutes until the dough is lightly toasted and the cheese has melted. Ovens vary in their intensity so keep an eye on it when you try this for the first time. If you're using a pizza oven the pizza can be placed directly onto the oven floor with a 'peel': a wide wooden or metal utensil that can support the whole pizza. Polenta scattered on the peel before placing your pizza will stop it sticking.

14. Blackcurrant jam

Fresh blackcurrants can be a little too taxing on the taste buds. Make jam from them and you have something that opens up all sorts of opportunities when it comes to sweetening things up. It's simply the most potent and memorable of aromas, a virtual time machine for anyone who picked blackcurrants as a child. Holding my head over a bubbling pan of blackcurrants and inhaling deeply is about as intoxicating as it gets in the kitchen.

450 g blackcurrants
340 g sugar
150 ml water

Remove stalks from blackcurrants and put into a pan with the water and boil together for 10 minutes. Add the sugar and then, once dissolved and boiling evenly, simmer for about 30 minutes or until the jam forms a skin when a little is poured on to a cold plate. Be careful to keep stirring the jam while it boils to keep it from burning and remove any scum that forms on the surface. Pour the jam into sterilised jars and fit airtight lids after it has cooled.

15. Beetroot and French bean salad

Another of our staples through the summer and both quick and simple to prepare. It's a somewhat reduced and garlicky version of a Nadine Abensur recipe (I think by now you can tell we like her recipes) which includes grilled haloumi, cumin seeds, balsamic vinegar and Tabasco.

Serves 2

300 g beetroot
150 g French beans, topped and tailed
1–2 cloves garlic, depending on how sociable you're feeling
3 tbsp extra virgin olive oil
a squeeze of lemon juice
sea salt and pepper to taste

Put whole beetroots into a pan of water. Be careful not to break their skins. Bring to a boil and then simmer for an hour. Rub the skins off and slice.

Cook the French beans in a pan of already boiling (slightly salted) water for 4–5 minutes so that they are firm to the bite but cooked through.

Finely slice the garlic and put into a bowl with the olive oil, lemon juice, salt and pepper. Throw in the beetroot and the beans and mix so that the vegetables are covered and serve.

16. Baked blackberry and stem ginger pudding

We are very fortunate in that Petersham Nurseries near Richmond-upon-Thames is just a bike ride away from where we live. They are famous not just as a fine and imaginative garden centre but also for the fact that Skye Gyngell runs the incredibly successful restaurant there. We've got into the habit of treating ourselves to a lunch there a week or so after exhibiting at Chelsea. In fact you could say that the *only* reason for exhibiting at Chelsea is so that we can feel sufficiently in need of a good spoiling afterwards.

This, perhaps our favourite autumn dessert, is from Skye's superb book, *A Year in My Kitchen*.

Serves 4

100 g unsalted butter, softened, with extra to grease
100 g caster sugar
2 organic free-range eggs
100 g self-raising flour
finely grated zest of 2 lemons
4 knobs of preserved stem ginger in syrup, drained and very finely chopped
a little pinch of salt
4 tbsp golden syrup
12 plump blackberries
thick Jersey cream

Preheat the oven to 180°C/350°F/gas mark 4. Butter 4 dariole moulds or individual pudding basins and set aside. Cream the softened butter and sugar together until pale and smooth. Add the eggs, one at a time, beating well after each addition. Sift in the flour from a good height and fold in gently. Finally, add the lemon zest, stem ginger and a restrained pinch of salt. Fold in until evenly mixed.

Put 1 tbsp golden syrup and 3 blackberries into each pudding mould and spoon the sponge mixture on top.

Cover each mould loosely with a piece of buttered foil and stand the moulds on a baking tray. Bake for 30 minutes until well risen and cooked through. To test, stick a skewer into the centre; it should come out clean.

Run a knife around each pudding and turn out onto a warm plate. Serve with a jug of rich, yellowy cream.
Note: Frozen summer fruit can be used well into winter and we occasionally swap the blackberries for blackcurrants or gooseberries.

17. Carrots braised with cumin, saffron and garlic

I'm very grateful to Nadine Abensur, who has let me use this recipe from her deliciously practical book, *The Cranks Bible*. It's such a simple dish, quick to prepare, and most importantly gives carrots the dignity they deserve as it brings out their natural sugars. It's a far cry from the overcooked, tasteless carrots of bygone schooldays, hospitals and in-flight meals.

Serves 4

500 g bunched carrots
4 tbsp olive oil
I tsp ground cumin
I tsp cumin seeds
150 ml water
a generous pinch of saffron
½ tsp Marigold vegetable bouillon stock powder
4 large or 6 small garlic cloves, finely sliced
a dash of Tabasco
sea salt and freshly ground black pepper
lemon wedges to serve

Wash the carrots and peel carefully, leaving the tops attached. If they are large, halve them lengthways, though not all the way so they stay attached at the top.

Place the carrots in a large saucepan (an oval cast iron pan is perfect) together with the olive oil, the ground cumin, cumin seeds, water, saffron, bouillon, garlic, salt, pepper and Tabasco. Make sure the carrots are lying as flat as possible in the pan and that they have all been doused in spicy oil.

Cover with a lid and simmer for about 20 minutes, checking occasionally to see that they are not sticking – though some catching on the bottom is a good thing as they should brown a little in places. Keep turning them over gently and shake the pot about now and again to distribute the flavours and the emerging sauce. Add a little water if it seems to be drying out too quickly. When they are ready, the tops will be completely wilted and the carrots covered in a sticky, saffron, garlic, cumin sauce. You will see carrots in a different light forever.

Serve with lemon wedges and either couscous or broad bean pilaf (see page 156).

18. Cavolo Nero with garlic and Parmesan

I must admit that I originally grew 'Cavolo Nero' kale for its looks rather than for its taste. Giuseppe advised me to cut out the central stem before cooking, which did make a difference, and then, ever since spotting this recipe by Skye Gyngell, it has been a firm favourite.

Serves 4–6

I kg Cavolo Nero
sea salt and freshly ground black pepper
100 g unsalted butter
I tbsp olive oil
I red onion, peeled and finely chopped
3 cloves garlic, peeled and finely chopped
150 g Parmesan cheese, freshly grated

Wash Cavolo Nero in cold water, then drain and cut out the tough white centre, leaving just the crinkly leaves.

Bring a large pan of well-salted water to the boil, add the Cavolo Nero and cook for 2 minutes after the water has returned to the boil. Drain and refresh under cold running water. Drain well.

In a separate pan, melt the butter with the olive oil and add the chopped onion, garlic, a generous pinch of salt and a good grinding of pepper. Sweat gently for 10 minutes until the onion is soft and translucent.

Add the Cavolo Nero and toss well to coat all the leaves in the garlicky butter. When warmed through, add the grated Parmesan, toss well and serve.

19. Broad bean pilaf with raisins and almonds

This is another recipe from Nadine Abensur and the ideal accompaniment to carrots braised with cumin, saffron and garlic (see above).

Serves 4

250 g basmati rice
200 g broad beans (you can use frozen but we use ours fresh from the plot)
2 tbsp olive oil
3–4 shallots, finely sliced
3 cloves garlic
1 tbsp cumin seeds
2 tbsp plump raisins
30 g whole almonds, sliced into fine slivers and toasted until pale gold
salt and freshly ground black pepper

Put the rice in a saucepan and cover with its volume in water. Bring to a boil but then quickly reduce to a simmer. Take it off the heat after around 14 minutes and keep the lid on for another 8 minutes so that it can steam in its own heat. This method produces a perfectly dry rice with independent grains, which will take the frying and stirring that's to follow without going mushy or falling apart.

At the moment you take the rice off the heat, bring some water to a boil in a separate pan. Add a little salt and boil broad beans for 8 minutes or so (they will be ready at the same time as the rice). Drain and refresh under cold running water and, if you have the patience, slip the bright green kernels from their tough grey-green skins.

Heat the oil in a large pan and fry the shallots (or onion if you have no shallots to hand) for 6 or 7 minutes until they are richly coloured and crisp in places. Stir pretty much continuously, adding the garlic about half-way through. (I don't add it in any earlier – in the heat required to turn the shallots their pale teak colour, the garlic has a tendency to burn.) And don't add salt until the shallots are done as it draws out the water and they end up boiling rather than frying and never turning brown at all. The cumin seeds go in for the last minute or so of well-stirred cooking.

Add the cooked rice, the broad beans and the raisins. Return to a safe heat and stir them together over and over, watching as the shallots lend a golden tinge to the rice. Sprinkle with almonds and serve.

20. Boston baked beans

Our American friend Julie may wonder why I've chosen this from all the amazing recipes she has up her sleeve. I think it's because it has 'allotment grub' written all over it. It's a very popular comfort food which is occasionally cooked at home and brought to eat with baked potatoes at the plot during the colder months.

Serves 8

200 g dried haricot beans
1 onion chopped
250 g black treacle
50 g muscovado sugar
110 g ketchup or tomato purée
1 tsp mustard powder
2 tsp salt
1 tbsp Worcestershire sauce
250 ml boiling water

Put haricot beans in a large bowl, cover with water and soak overnight or for 8–12 hours. Drain beans, then cover with fresh water and simmer on a low heat until cooked through (approx. 45 mins–1 hour). Add beans to a casserole dish with the rest of the ingredients. Mix well, then cover and bake in oven at 150°C/300°F/gas mark 2 for 6–7 hours. Check every 2 hours (add water if necessary) and cook uncovered for the last hour.

21. Baked pears with honey, marsala and bay

It seems incredible that you should do anything to a pear other than eat it ripe and uncooked with the juice running down the side of your mouth. However, this recipe from Skye Gyngell is a wonderful winter warmer. I didn't have any honey in the larder so substituted brown sugar and added some nuts for the picture below.

Serves 6–8
8 firm ripe pears (Martin Sec, Comice or Conference)
600 ml marsala
220 ml fragrant honey
1 cinnamon stick
1 vanilla pod, split lengthways
finely pared zest of 1 lemon
sprig of bay leaves (4 or 5 leaves)

Preheat oven to 200°C/400°F/gas mark 6. Place pears in a roasting dish in which they fit quite snugly with their stalks uppermost. Pour over the marsala and drizzle over the honey, then add the cinnamon stick, vanilla pod, lemon zest and bay leaves. Cover the dish tightly with foil.

Place the roasting dish on the middle shelf of the oven and roast for 20 minutes. Remove the foil and bake, uncovered, for a further 20 minutes. The pears should be soft and the skin slightly wrinkly.

Serve the pears warm (not hot) on individual plates with the marsala and honey syrup spooned over. Add crème fraiche or vanilla ice cream if you fancy but they are good enough on their own.

CHAPTER ELEVEN

The future

Christine is a firm believer in living in the present and making the best of things, but writing this book has made me wonder about the significance of the Grow Your Own movement and where it might lead. Trends come and go in the world of horticulture. The honeymoon phase for allotments may be over in terms of their not being front page news any more, but the movement wasn't just a flash in the pan and has settled nicely into the world of horticulture as a permanent fixture. The knock-on effects have already been felt in schools and community spaces, which have helped to offset some of the frustration of waiting lists, and the emphasis on locally produced food is reaching a much wider audience.

We have become so comfortable with a lifestyle of convenience that it is unthinkable it will ever be any different

Without wanting to sound too dramatic, the drive towards the notion of self-sufficiency might play an important part in shaping attitudes towards a more sustainable future in which communities rely more heavily on their food being produced locally. It has set many people wondering just what lies in store for the human race once our most precious resources run out.

Peak oil

Peak oil refers to the period when the maximum rate of petroleum extraction is achieved worldwide and after which the rate of production diminishes in terminal decline. You don't need to be a scientist to work out that our current way of life is unsustainable. Once oil runs out, everything from travel and heating to petrochemical products such as household appliances and computers will be affected. Much of this we take for granted but unless an alternative energy source, as easily available and affordable, is discovered soon, current lifestyles and economies will have to change and adapt dramatically as the effects of reduced oil supplies are felt globally.

Exactly what this means for future generations isn't at all clear. Current research based on present consumption rates suggest that available oil reserves will last until 2030 and natural gas until 2060. Some scientists believe that the risks taken in the Gulf of Mexico which led to the BP Deepwater Horizon oil disaster in 2010 clearly indicate that we have already entered a state of peak oil.

Predictions such as these are, on the face of it, gloomy. We have become so comfortable with a lifestyle of convenience that it is unthinkable it will ever be any different. The human race is apprehensive of change at the best of times and will undoubtedly have difficulty coming to terms with a future without the opportunities

Just before going to press, a rumour that allotment rents are set to skyrocket has got many people a-worrying that they might not be able to afford the plots that they have spent much of their lives on. The future, for some, is uncertain.

and luxuries of the oil age. We are also, let's face it, a selfish species and rarely consider the needs of generations beyond our grandchildren.

But dramatic lifestyle changes *will* happen, maybe not in our lifetime, but sooner or later things will change and it's only fair to future generations that we get used to the idea and do something to prepare for it, even if it's only changing our attitude to soften the blow. Potential hardships can be made easier by accepting the inevitable, taking a more positive outlook and seeing the benefits. Communities will become closer and, to a large degree, more dependent on local food, products and services. Families will be less likely to move long distances from each other. OK, some people might hate the thought of their families living closer, but if travel does become a major issue then it will almost certainly have a bearing on the geography of future generations.

To some this may seem like going backwards, a return to an almost medieval culture or something akin to the post-apocalyptic future portrayed in the film *Mad Max*. But it needn't be that bad. We just have to get used to the idea that change is on the way and the sooner we start accepting it, the easier the transition will be. Much will depend on how we adapt to having. This is no bad thing. We have enjoyed the richest of times and much of it at the expense of deforestation, exploitation of resources and cheap labour abroad. It would be madness to think that it would last for ever.

But we have also learned a great deal, especially about our dependence on nature and that with a little thought and foresight we can create sustainable landscapes and habitats rich in biodiversity. By taking more notice of the events that are happening in our immediate locality, we can start to build stronger communities that will be well equipped to deal with whatever comes their way. Engaging with like-minded folk and strengthening links with food-growers, beekeepers, farmers and craftsmen will become increasingly important. We will also value the importance of saving our own seed.

Until fairly recently, the majority of gardeners and farmers around the world saved their own seed: seed that would have been peculiar to their own region for hundreds of years and therefore more suited to the local soil and climate and less susceptible to disease. The advent of modern hybrids and genetically modified seed has almost destroyed this valuable resource and has made the world reliant on modern farming techniques that, in turn, are completely reliant on oil. What's more, hybrids are not always bred to be better in terms of taste or higher yield; one of the main drivers is uniformity – to make harvesting and packing more efficient and to make them all the more alluring on supermarket shelves.

It's a complicated process and could warrant a book in itself but, in a nutshell, F1 seed is produced by crossing two unrelated parental lines. The offspring will carry the traits of each parent plant such as taste, colour, yield or disease resistance. So, for example, if one tomato, known for its taste but susceptibility to blight, is crossed with another that shows more blight resistance, with a bit of luck the offspring (the F1 generation) will carry both the taste characteristic of one parent and the disease resistance of the other. There are no guarantees and it can be a long process, hence the inflated price of F1 seed. The downside is that seed saved from F1 varieties won't grow true to type so you have to buy your seed for the following season.

On a large scale, hybrids have undoubtedly helped farmers with improved yields and reliability; on a small scale gardeners benefit not only from the predictability but also from new varieties that come onto the market each year. The danger is that we rely too heavily on F1s at the expense of heirloom seed where strong gene pools are ensured. If open-pollinated heirloom seeds disappear, we lose genetic diversity and that could spell disaster for future generations.

Fortunately there are pockets of knowledge like The Real Seed Catalogue (www.realseeds.co.uk), which not only supplies real seed but also tells you how to collect it yourself. This might seem bonkers in terms of business sense, but companies like this may well turn out to be a lifeline when it comes to preserving our seed heritage.

If nothing else, our plot has taught us that the old cliché, *The best things in life are free'*, is not far off the truth. I'm as bad as anyone else in terms of hankering after the next iPhone, iPad or gadget that is meant to simplify our lives, but time spent at the plot without having to be a slave to technology is enriching and wholesome. The upsurge of interest in allotments and growing food, therefore, may well empower people to be resourceful when it comes to food. What we currently consider as an interesting pastime could be crucial in helping future generations be creative in terms of food production and making the best of local resources.

Relying too heavily on F1 hybrids to make tomato blight (above) and other diseases a thing of the past could put genetic diversity under threat.

Should the worst predictions (restricted travel, reduced imports and expensive commodities) come true, the Grow Your Own revival could become one of the most important movements in garden history and, in a worst-case scenario, the very lynchpin of future agrarian societies. As bleak and pessimistic as it sounds, if we can at least begin to talk about the post-oil era before it happens, it will help nations prepare for the transitional phase and soften the blow when it does fall. Arming people with the knowledge they need for the changes could help offset anxiety and even conflict if mass unemployment, homelessness, famine and disease loom on a bleak horizon. In short, the fun we're having on allotments now might one day provide our children with the most vital lifeline of the modern era.

Sorry, I had no idea that writing about allotments was going to be so serious.

Common Ground

One of the best lectures I've ever had the pleasure of attending was some twenty years ago and given by Sue Clifford, co-founder of Common Ground, the charity that champions local distinctiveness. Customs, orchards and all things peculiar to the English way of life enrich our lives, often without our being aware of them. These things we take for granted are so familiar that we don't always notice them until they've gone.

'The knowledge of scientists is different from vernacular understanding. We need both. Particularly we need to value and keep wisdom practised in its place.

Indigenous knowledge, intangible benefits, subjective perceptions, emotional attachments and expressions of value need other languages and other champions.'

The Common Ground Book of Orchards

The work of Common Ground has done much to preserve the kind of fabric of life in this country which is so difficult to quantify, cost or substitute.

Allotments are part of this complex fabric and should be preserved at all costs. Developers once saw them as cash cows. Fortunately the surge of interest at the beginning of this millennium has thwarted many attempts to exploit them. Some councils have even found themselves in the awkward position of not only conserving what they have but also looking for more land for people eager to try their hand at growing their own food.

The simplest way of boosting and accentuating local distinctiveness is to celebrate places and customs with events like fêtes and open days. Common Ground started Apple Day, a nationwide celebration of the value of orchards and their place in society through work, leisure, biodiversity and conservation. With 60 per cent of orchards having disappeared since the 1950s, Apple Day has helped raise awareness for the remaining jewels that pepper our towns and villages and has even inspired new ones. People are left to interpret and celebrate in any way they see fit, and orchards, potent in their symbolism, are perfect places to host such events. So too are allotments.

Something our events committee has pondered is a revival of an old May Day custom to celebrate the mischievous symbol of fertility, the Green Man. The foliate face of the Green Man can often be seen in the vaults and pews of churches and cathedrals throughout the UK. Pictures and sculptures depict him disgorging foliage and he comes in various guises from Jack in the Green to Robin Hood, depending on your location.

Traditionally, on May Day, someone would be chosen to dress up as the Green Man and front a parade where debauched licentious behaviour, often fuelled by a few yards of ale, was par for the course. It's potentially a much more difficult thing to sell to other plot-holders at Bushy Park as pagan lore isn't widely celebrated these days. The need to call upon Nature, God or whatever you want to call it for favourable weather and then give thanks to celebrate the harvest was once a matter of survival; it wasn't just fun, it actually meant something. Today we take it for granted that if our potatoes get blight we have the supermarket as back-up. This is a pity as celebrations to mark the seasons can be incredibly potent milestones in people's lives that can help us keep a grip on the passing of time, and besides, if nothing else, Henry would make a damn fine Green Man and he knows it.

With a young orchard at the back of Bushy Park Allotment Association's community plot, wassailing might be an easier option. Peculiar to the cider regions of the country, wassailing involves singing, drinking and anointing orchards with cider to ensure a good harvest for the coming season. A Malt House that once produced ale and mead for Hampton Court Palace sits just over the fence from the allotment, so perhaps this

16th July 2010
Joanna Fortnam at the Telegraph asked me today if I'd be interested in designing their show garden at the Chelsea Flower Show. Feeling very fortunate to be asked but know that this will impact on the allotment in a big way next year. April and May are critical months in getting things planted at the plot but Chelsea takes up all our time. Julie and David helped me out last time. I wonder if they'll have time to help me out again?

Sculpted columns by Serge Bottagisio and Agnes Decoux have featured in three of my gardens at the Chelsea Flower Show.

Despite my allergy to the fruit, we have planted over ten apple trees at our plot. Through the good work of the charity Common Ground orchards have become a metaphor for a way of life that is so enriching.

ought to be the shoe-in to revive such a celebration. With all the spare apples from the allotments we could even have a go at making cider. While it might sound interesting enough to be worth a try, getting it off the ground might prove a little more difficult. Preserving and perpetuating customs that have been practised for generations is one thing; the reinstatement or inception of a tradition, especially in a place that has no history of getting drunk and dancing around apple trees in the altogether, is liable to get us arrested.

Open days have been by far the best way of engaging with the local community. Traditionally, Bushy Park Allotment Association hosts two open days each year: a plant sale in spring and a harvest festival in late summer. Some think that it's just an excuse to eat an awful lot of cake and, to a large extent, they'd be right, but open days are a useful vehicle for bringing allotments to the wider attention of the local community. Some visitors, despite having lived in the locality for years, have never seen inside the allotment walls and are pleasantly surprised to see what they have on their doorstep. It helps strengthen the identity of the area and lend a sense of community, not just within the allotment itself but as a landmark in the local town of Hampton. It might seem like a small thing, insignificant even, but it's often the small things that make all the difference in communities and are therefore the things to keep alive.

While I was writing this book, organisers of the first ever Hampton Hill Summer Festival asked us to join in by opening our gates as part of the celebration and, having found myself on the events subcommittee along with Sainsbury's John and Ted, it seemed ungracious not to agree. Bethan, a local schoolteacher and plot-holder, welcomes local schoolchildren and Brownie groups to the plot. With John and Henry to help, they are shown what goes on within the allotment walls and given tips for starting a veg patch of their own. Local art groups occasionally spend the whole day at the plot with their easels and find plenty to inspire them.

Our plot sometimes seems a world away from the gardens I design for clients and flower shows. The common denominator of course is plants. Show gardens and private gardens may be more theatrical or geared towards a different lifestyle but the joy of growing things and the ability to beautify space

and make a positive contribution to biodiversity is not a bad way to earn a living. If nothing else, the allotment reminds us that a garden is never finished. It shifts and changes from season to season, year to year. Nothing remains the same. Amen to that.

Open days are an effective way of engaging with the local community and connecting people.

Allotments may have peaked in terms of newsworthiness but, as time goes on and as resources become scarce, they may well increase their standing in the community and find themselves enjoying further periods of renaissance when locally sourced food becomes more a necessity than a token of half-hearted commitment to the notion of sustainability.

Manor Garden Allotments

Not as multicultural as some inner-city allotments, Bushy Park Allotment Association still has a reasonable mix of nationalities that are characteristic of allotment culture in this country. Vietnam, China, Madeira, Jamaica, America and Italy are represented and it's all the richer for it. It's widely recognised that allotments are microcosms where age, class, gender, race, colour and creed can integrate freely. It could be argued that allotments exist as a model of a utopian existence and nowhere was this expressed more clearly than at Manor Garden Allotments in the Lea Valley, one of the most potent examples of urban greening I'd ever seen.

Juliet Roberts, editor of *Gardens Illustrated*, introduced us to it. She had gardened there with her friend, Julie Sumner, for some years but in 2006 this nugget of green within the raw industrial landscape of East London was facing demolition to make way for footpaths and landscaping at the 2012 London Olympics. Sport had been my world as a youth, gardening consumes me now. Here was a story where I could relate to both sides of the fence but one that left me wondering whether noble virtues, Olympian virtues no less, were things of the past.

The allotments had been established by Major Arthur Villiers, Old Etonian, philanthropist and director of Barings Bank, through the The Manor Charitable Trust (now Villiers Park Educational Trust) which was formed in 1924 by him and three

31st October 2010

Phil has just brought me a laminated sheet with a list of seeds he is planning to bring to next week's AGM where he is organising a seed swap. He has a fine selection: bunching onions, beans, cucumber, parsnip, mustard, peas and tomatoes, some of which he's saved himself. Apart from parsnips, I haven't saved any seed this year and take all the half-empty packets home to sort for the big day. To my amazement and annoyance I find a large, unopened envelope from The Real Seed Catalogue that had fallen behind the box where the seeds are kept. Inside are 24 packets of seed that didn't even see the light of day this season. Cavolo nero, three types of squash I'd never grown before, exploding cucumber and quinoa, a novelty grain I wanted to try since seeing some growing on Phil's plot. I get over it quickly. It's been a distracting year. Most of it will keep for next season so at least I've saved myself some money, even though it might be at the expense of making this book and our kitchen more interesting.

other Old Etonians (Gerald Wellesley, Alfred Wagg and Sir Edward Cadogan). Villiers, a friend of Winston Churchill, was so disgusted by the way the working class were treated, both on the battlefields of the First World War and when they returned home, that he donated land in and around the Lea Valley, and created sports facilities for deprived children and allotments for their families on which to grow food. When London won the Olympic bid and news came that the allotments would have to go to make way for a concourse for the four-week event, Julie Sumner and fellow plot-holders mounted a campaign to save one hundred years of history from being wiped out at a stroke. However, the link between sport and locally grown food, once seen as an essential ingredient for healthy living at Manor Gardens, wasn't enough to save the allotments from being bulldozed to make way for 'the greenest Olympics ever'.

The true cost of the London Olympics may never be known. The millions spent on land remediation to neutralise toxic waste that had lain dormant (and probably less harmful) for over a century is staggering in comparison to what it would have cost to incorporate Manor Garden Allotments into the overall scheme. Not linking the two not only extinguished a thriving community and the aspirations of one of the most respected philanthropists of his day, but was also an elementary gaffe in terms of sensitive and sustainable design. Any landscape design student worth their salt would have made the historical link and exploited the opportunity to make Manor Garden a shining example of the Olympic ideal.

This lack of vision was probably based on the planners' assumption that people wouldn't be able to 'see' the historical connection and that they wouldn't stomach the contrast where, on the face of it, shanty town meets the sleek and shiny modern world. But the contrast to the landscaped areas would have been a masterstroke and a beacon symbolising friendship, cooperation, tolerance, and understanding: Olympian virtues no less.

The opening ceremony for the Beijing Olympics in 2008 raised the bar so high for subsequent host nations that organisers of the London Olympics understandably refused to try and compete with it. When accepting the role as choreographer for the opening ceremony, Oscar-winning film director, Danny Boyle said that he would 'stage the event to highlight Britain's "idiosyncrasies" and to showcase London as "a welcoming city without prejudice"'. Idiosyncrasy isn't displayed anywhere more clearly than at an allotment. Manor Garden Allotments, to my mind, would have been Danny's trump card. The London Olympics simply missed a trick.

Farmers' markets

Local farmers' markets set the pace and will be an importance source of information if some of the aforementioned predictions come true. Farmers grow for a living and have valuable knowledge peculiar to each locality. But at the height of the Grow Your Own craze a few people expressed concern for market gardeners and whether the new climate of self-sufficiency would adversely affect business. It's something I had never considered before, but it made sense to be concerned for local food producers whose businesses might be affected and even destabilised by people trying their hand at the good life.

Iain Tolhurst of Tolhurst Organic Produce agreed that there was a general feeling that producers supplying veg boxes had indeed suffered from the allotment boom. With a customer base showing a natural inclination to grow their own, it was difficult to put an accurate figure on how many customers had left, but it had been a significant percentage with many of his colleagues sharing similar stories. 'Obviously it is not something we particularly like,' said Tolly. 'But I am in favour of people growing their own where they can. We fill the gaps where they can't and we may end up concentrating more on staple bulky crops and less on summer salad types.' This is borne out by customers who return come October during the leaner months for potatoes, brassicas and other staples that take up too much space on allotments and private gardens. 'Some will realise that it is just not worth the effort and give up, hopefully returning to us.'

I think this is exactly what will happen. Allotments are a bit like going to the gym. Making the initial effort to go for a workout is always the main hurdle. Once in the zone and working up a sweat it's the best place in the world. The owners of gymnasiums throughout the world know that if all their members turned up every day there would be no room to move. But they understand human nature only too well and rely on the simple fact that most people haven't got the staying power. There may well be waiting lists for allotments but they are always in a state of flux as people eventually realise just what's involved in growing food.

The future of 'Our Plot'

Like most gardeners we are always looking to improve things and we experiment at the allotment. Ideas evolve and change from year to year and this helps to keep the place vital enough to hold our interest. The following is a list of some of the things on the back burner.

Livestock

As I'd looked after hens as a teenager, it was natural to become broody once several people at the plot started keeping hens. I also fancied keeping bees, having had a little experience through a family friend – appropriately named – Mr Waxman. At the time of writing, however – tempting as it was to make this book more wholesome with pictures of us with feathery creatures and cooing over dripping honeycombs – we are both concerned about the extra time that would be needed to keep the hens in good health.

Hens

If the idea of keeping chickens appeals to you, it's worth checking with your local council first as to whether you can keep livestock. If you are allowed to, then particular attention should be paid to where you intend to keep them and how you plan to

While livestock is becoming increasingly popular these days on some allotments, we know that the extra time needed to commit to animal welfare is unrealistic for us just now.

keep them secure. Easy access, shelter and security are the three most important considerations when siting a chicken run. It's also worth bearing in mind that hens can be very destructive on an allotment and, while the notion of them having a generous free range is a noble one, it's not necessarily the most practical. It really is best to keep them in a chicken run but hang on to the thought that they will be in conditions infinitely better than battery hens. If you have a fenced-in plot then you could, occasionally, let the hens out into the wider garden where they'll do a good job in picking out slugs and snails. Don't leave them out too long, however; otherwise they'll scratch where you don't want them to and you'll even think more kindly about pigeons if you let hens anywhere near your brassicas.

An appropriate amount of time needs to be spent on livestock to keep it so. It is a commitment and needs attention on a daily basis if it is to be kept fed and watered.

Traditional chicken houses are made from timber and come in all sorts of guises from simple shed-like structures to more elaborate 'houses' verging on the twee. Timber blends well in any situation and particularly at an allotment. They can be bought in kit form and assembled on site, but many people choose to make their own using either new timber or reclaimed wood. Cleanliness is paramount when making a hen house and rotting timber can provide homes for mites and be difficult to clean.

The modern Eglu, made from plastic, has removable sides, easy-hose surfaces, insulation and wheels so the coop can be

10th June 2010

An early morning session at the plot. Finding most of our lettuce seedlings demolished overnight I have reached a quiet resolve to do something drastic. I fill a 3-litre pot almost to the brim with slugs and snails that are hiding under logs and enjoying the humid spots where weeds and long grass make an ideal habitat for them next to the raised beds. Instead of depositing them on the other side of the stream I take them to Giuseppe's plot and feed them to his hens. They almost wet themselves with excitement and make quick work of this unexpected breakfast. I don't feel particularly good or bad about it. More resigned and frustrated that I've had to resort to killing things, albeit in a roundabout way.

moved. It also has a fox-proof mesh run to keep your hens secure. Hugely popular, they are perhaps a little too slick-looking for an allotment.

Giuseppe's first hens were rescued from a battery farm. They looked in a sorry state, featherless, scarred and scared out of their wits when they first arrived, but gradually they adapted to their new-found freedom and eventually grew back their feathers. There's a chance that battery hens, with the stresses and trauma of their confinement, might be more feisty and even aggressive than modern pure breeds but this is a noble gesture to give them just a little respite from a short tough life.

I was very eager to get my own chickens while I was writing this book. My mother had plans to move house to be near the allotment and this would have made it a reality as we could have shared the responsibility. Since her passing I have been less enthusiastic and while Kathy, out neighbour, likes the idea of hens and has kindly offered to help care for them, this idea is still on the back burner. We haven't ruled it out but the commitment hasn't been made yet.

Bees

Colony Collapse Disorder (CCD) has caused the loss of a quarter of a million hives in the UK, a third of all the hives in the country. It's hard to imagine that the extinction of an insect could have a cataclysmic effect on the planet with far worse implications than depleted oil reserves but, if bees die out, shortages in some areas of food production would almost certainly follow. While plant life would undoubtedly be affected to some degree, it is unclear just how a mass extinction of bees would affect the world's food supply. Fruit would be most under threat. Cherry, apple and pear species would undoubtedly be affected, as would any plant relying on bee pollination to bear seed.

Tuberous ground crops such as potatoes wouldn't be threatened; neither would wind-pollinated crops such as maize and other cereals. There are also many other insects that pollinate flowers. Wasps, hoverflies and even houseflies are attracted to nectar but not on the scale that bees are. Should the honeybee die out, populations of these other insects together with those of solitary bees might well increase to fill the gap. Another hope is that populations of bees resistant to varroa, the most common disease affecting them, would increase in time, but this is mostly speculation and it's safe to assume that without the honeybee food production would face some sort of crisis.

Beekeeping has therefore never been more popular. I was told that I would have to wait a year to get onto a local beekeeping course and have since explored the idea of providing a site for a local apiarist on our plot. Plot-holders who have kept bees at Bushy Park allotments have had their hives affected by CCD. Some years are worse than others. But they persist in trying to establish new colonies.

Again it's worth checking with your local authority before you invest in an apiary, and consideration must be given to neighbouring plot-holders who are either scared of bees or allergic to their sting. If, for whatever reason, you can't keep bees, there is a British Beekeepers Association (BBKA) scheme whereby people can help the plight of the humble bee by adopting a beehive. Money raised from sponsoring a hive will fund

The plight of the humble bee has caused a resurgence of interest in bee-keeping.

research into honeybee health and educational programmes for beekeepers.
http://www.adoptabeehive.co.uk/

Eco-loo

There are 385 plots at the Bushy Park allotments and one portaloo. To date I've never
used it, preferring instead to pee into a bucket and use the urea on brassicas or the
compost heap. Many people, however, are too shy to share their emissions, which is
a shame and a waste. They are even more sensitive about big-jobs, number twos or
whatever you want to call it.

I've been hesitant to use 'night soil' largely because it involves a bit of organisation
and diligence with the whole process if it is to be performed safely. Night soil is a
euphemism for human faeces, once collected (at night, which of course gave it its
name) by gong farmers during the sixteenth century, and later by honeypot men in the
nineteenth century. It has been used most regularly by Chinese and Indian cultures in
the past and was used in the UK as recently as the Second World War when fertilisers
for home-grown food were scarce. Today, as we question our environmental record
and what we can do to improve it, the use of night soil in our gardens remains, as far
as I can make out, an untapped resource largely because we are too squeamish.

Pathogens in improperly or incompletely composted human faeces can be hazardous,
so too can chemicals that find their way into our sewerage systems. However, organic
waste recyclers, such as Terra-Ecosystems, have for some years been using sewage
sludge, together with woodchip and other green material, to make safe compost to
use in our gardens. Home waste recycling can also reduce the hazards so long as the
right processes are adopted and the sewage is given adequate time to decompose
completely (about a year in the UK). As a safeguard, fertiliser made from home waste
should only be used on fruit crops and not salads where there is the risk of direct
contact with the fertiliser.

The all-singing, all-dancing self-contained composting toilets (www.composting
toilet.org) have a large compartment below the toilet with a sophisticated aeration
system. Other, smaller systems as advocated by Joseph Jenkins in *The Humanure Handbook*
serve only to prepare the waste for a secondary composting in a regular compost heap.
Jenkins, who coined the neologism 'humanure', advocates using all household and
sanitary waste, believing that rather than being a risk it can actually improve public
health and safety. Not only will you reap the benefits in the garden, you will also be
saving around 75,000 gallons of water a year by not having to flush.

We did think of commissioning the sculptor Johnny Woodford to make one of
his portable loo-cum-sedans (with a wood-shaving flush) that add a touch of class
and portability to your regular thunderbox. A high water table at our plot makes this
impractical but I'm pleased to report that an eco-loo is currently being considered by
the allotment committee.

Alternative energy

Other than on open days there isn't a huge demand for electricity at the allotment. All
the same, alternative energy is often a topic of conversation. Solar and wind power are

obvious areas to explore but my experience is that the technology is limiting in terms of output and is expensive to set up. Generators and propane gas burners do for most of our energy needs but it would be interesting to experiment with solar cookers. Simple in principle, box and funnel cookers use mirrors or aluminium reflectors to concentrate sunlight along a line to heat vessels within them. Cheap and easy to construct, they are a godsend to people who must burn firewood every day to cook their food. The devices will reduce illnesses caused by smoke, reduce deforestation and stop women and children from having to spend much time collecting the fuel (often leaving them exposed to danger). The only downside is that it makes my earth oven seem very wasteful by comparison. http://www.solarcooking.org/

Conclusion

As a garden designer I do my utmost to create spaces that resonate with their surroundings rather than slavishly following a trend. Growing food is more of a movement than a trend, but it's inevitable that now the honeymoon period is over there will be fewer headlines about allotments and vegetable gardens in the gardening media. That doesn't mean that it will go away. It's true that many people beguiled by the promise of the good life have had a rude awakening when confronted by the amount of time and energy it takes to grow their own food, but equally there are plenty of people, families and communities who have found the whole experience of food production an enriching experience and one they are now wedded to embracing, not as a fad to crow about but as part of their daily or weekly routine.

While a big part of me wants to continue creating gardens that are purely aesthetic and a million miles from the scruffy nature of allotments and food production, I am sure that the Grow Your Own movement is timely and that we may well be practising for a tenuous future where food production may one day become a matter of survival.

Straddling these two worlds can, at times, seem like the ultimate paradox, so it's encouraging when other designers pick up the baton. The kitchen gardens at West Dean, Great Dixter and Chatsworth are more absorbing than ever and, encouragingly, Kim Wilkie, one of Britain's leading contemporary designers, has proposed a scheme of orchards and vegetable plots for the site of the now demolished Chelsea Barracks. Set in one of the most expensive developments in London, it's seen by estate agents as a ridiculous proposal but to my mind it is audacious and visionary.

Each passing year reinforces our bond with the plot and we consider ourselves fortunate to have such a space where we can imagine that we're not just three miles from home but at a country retreat. I often wonder whether we would be quite so enthusiastic if our plot was surrounded by buildings as some allotments are. Possibly not, but I think people tend to make the best of their situation wherever it is, especially these days now that allotments are scarce. The amount of time invested in keeping our plot productive and in order can be overwhelming but it still carries enough magic to keep us coming back for more.

The year during which this book was written was, more than anything else, a lesson in learning that we should cherish what we have. Our enjoyment has come as much from the social side of the allotment – reinventing the notion of 'community' – as from growing food. It had become a happy place for family and friends to visit and to relive some of what I felt to have been lost over the years. My mother's passing, however, just at a time when she was about to move closer to the plot, was a sucker-punch. It's taken something precious away and has, if I'm honest, made me seriously consider how long we might keep the plot. As we all learn at some time in our lives, you can't have everything and nothing lasts forever.

Time and not being able to police the plot remain our main concerns and, if we are to stay, a more organised approach with more permanent crops like fruit and herbs will be necessary. To that end we have made some progress at least. Espaliered apples and pears already bring structure to the plot, and new fruit trees including cider apples and even a mulberry (though at the time of writing I've no clue as to where to plant it) have been ordered to mark our commitment to the place, just as we did a decade ago.

So the book simply marks our efforts on a patch of ground we had tentatively acquired a decade ago. It's nothing to do with being an expert in growing food. In fact I would say that most people we've met who grow their own have far more success than we do. Much of this has to do with the fact that we are time poor and can't quite get over killing things, but the simple truth remains that I'm much better at designing gardens than I am at growing food. 'Charles Dowding or Mark Diacono know far more than me!' I say in a fit of anxiety every time someone asks me to give a talk about our perceived good life. It's not my comfort zone but if I do speak, I tell it as I have here. It's the true picture. But allotments are also what you make of them. They may well be time consuming, difficult, frustrating and much hard work, but they are also magical, some of the most precious gems we have in the world of horticulture, and may turn out to be a vital cog in how we shape the communities of the future. Fashionable or not, these scraps of land are priceless and should be venerated, celebrated and preserved.

CHAPTER TWELVE

Mum

Regular family gatherings were suddenly history. I don't think we really appreciated just how special it was at the time.

My mother, Yvette, was born in Calcutta, India. She came to the UK along with the rest of her Anglo-Indian family when things got too hot for comfort during partition. Times were hard for this uprooted family which had been used to quite a high standard of living in Bengal, so each member of the family pooled their resources as employment was found. Being the first Anglo-Indians to arrive on British soil was a daunting experience, but Mum and some of her equally good-looking friends were fortunate to find well-paid employment as extras at Pinewood Film Studios, with a virtual monopoly in films where dark-skinned, scantily clad hoolah-hoolah girls were needed.[1] Most of the family found work on the set of *Bowhani Junction*, my grandmother, Vida, playing the part of Ava Gardner's mother (see onion bhajee recipe on page 143).

By the time I showed up in 1958 we lived on Thames Ditton Island, but the hub of family life was my grandmother's home in Harrow where most of the family would gather every Saturday. The kitchen was a hive of activity where Gran and most of the women in the family caught up with the week's events while stirring steaming degchis of dal, rice and curries and watching kuris of hot oil splutter forth delicious onion bhajees and samosas. The smell of these staples filled the house (and more than likely the street) and fed what seemed like the whole family throughout the day. Every Saturday.

Eventually, as they married and had children, the family, like many families in the UK, fragmented as they moved to different parts of the country. In 1972 Gran sold her house to help my parents buy the Lorna Doone Hotel in Porlock, Somerset, and the regular family gatherings were suddenly history. I don't think we really appreciated just how special it was at the time. The family were naturally doing what every Anglo-Indian family would do anywhere. It wasn't a big deal. The attraction of owning their own homes and moving to different parts of the world seemed natural, too, as each family sought their own independence and as the pace of the world around them gathered speed. As I've got older I've come to realise just how lucky we were to have had such a close-knit upbringing.

---

[1] Most of these were Norman Wisdom films, notably *Man of the Moment* (1955).

LEFT An early, but uninspiring, encounter with a dandelion at the age of three.
RIGHT Mum, with me aged 4 months.

Today, our relatives are still scattered – some have even emigrated – so the sense of 'family' bears little resemblance to those days. But the allotment, in some respects, has done something to fill this void. In some small way the allotment can, if you let it, become a centre. A place where people with a common interest can gather. Of course it will never come close to replacing what we once had but, in the broadest sense of the word, there is a sort of kinship, which is vibrant and healthy.

Mum must have felt this potential early on as she was besotted with the allotment. She and her husband, Larry, loved nothing more than spending time with us there where life is at its simplest best. Her capacity for fun and revelry meant she was always on call to help fetch and carry (and there's a lot of that at an allotment), cook and clear up – more often than not by candlelight. On open days she worked tirelessly to make the day a success and took enormous pride and satisfaction in keeping the plot in order if ever we were away for any length of time. In fact, while most allotment holders would never see the sense in taking a holiday during the growing season, we found it to our advantage. Mum and Larry achieved more in two weeks than we could ever manage in a month. The first port of call on the way back from a holiday was always the allotment so they could proudly show us all the things they had got up to while we'd been away. Twice I spoiled her moment. Once when someone ignored the rules of engagement on a roundabout just a mile or two from home and the second on returning from Nepal with a stowaway in my liver. Her first concern was obviously my health in both cases, but I felt her disappointment that we couldn't rush straight to the allotment and marvel (and I mean properly marvel, not pretend) at the work they had achieved while we had been away.

Her sudden and unexpected death,[2] a month or two into writing this book, was devastating. Just four weeks earlier she had been weeding the raised beds, helping me put the finishing touches to a short film about the plot and having enormous fun putting the first layer of clay on our earth oven. We talked about the plan to move

---

[2] A medical misadventure following, as it turned out, unnecessary exploratory surgery.

6th March 2010

A cold bright day with an icy wind. An important day as we're building the first layer of mud for the earth oven. Mum and Larry arrive. Their first visit of the year. Mum's keen to get stuck in, but first I film her digging the front border in a large floppy hat, so I can add a comic touch to a short film I'm making about bindweed. The hat is the same one she wore when she came to see my first show garden at Hampton Court and she spends most of the time trying to stop the wind from blowing it to Hampton Court Palace. We don wellies and tread sharp sand into the clay which will help stop it from cracking. Hard work. Much laughter as it's the most inelegant task I've ever given my mother. We then mould the clay around a mound of sharp sand which will leave the void when it's removed once the clay dries. Mum opts for gloves but I like the feel of the clay as there's something so beautifully honest and satisfying about working with mud. For a while we work in silence, building the dome that we know will soon become the hearth of the plot. Mum is in her element and now even more keen to move house to be nearer the plot. I don't think I've ever enjoyed a day quite so much.

24th April 2010

Take my brother and his family to Heathrow. They are relieved to be going home at last now that the ash from Mount Eyjafjallajokull has allowed flights to return to normal, but I dread them going. Their early departure means I get to the allotment early enough to help set up for the plant sale. Due to the events of the past few weeks I haven't done anything to organise it, but Giuseppe is already there setting up stalls and soon others come to help. Seedlings, plants and old tools, not to mention tea and cake, will help raise money for the allotment shop. The day goes like clockwork and the weather is, once again, kind to us. It feels like a dream but we're happy to be there.

house from Shoreham-by-Sea to Hampton to be nearer us, and the plot. This was going to be the year. It was one of those perfect days you cherish for ever but made even more poignant now as it turned out to be the last time we would ever work together at the plot.

The significance of her dying on April 2nd can only really be appreciated by those who grow their own food. April, regardless of whether you have a book to write or not, is a crucial month in the vegetable garden. Beds (neglected through too much attention being paid to the earth oven) needed more preparation, seeds needed sowing and perversely enough, with no April showers, there was watering to be done. Grief, however, trivialises everything and for a month the allotment languished. 'Our Plot' was the last thing on my mind and the silence brought about by the Easter break with no planes taking off from Heathrow seemed not so much an inconvenience as an appropriate mark of respect.

As it turned out, 2010 was a distressing year for many at the allotment with Giuseppe and Stefan (another allotment friend) losing their mothers and Christine losing her brother. We have all found some measure of solace at the plot and have been grateful for something to focus on. Being one of those cringingly proud mothers, I know that she was already looking forward to seeing *Our Plot* being published and I've no doubt that she had a hat in mind for the book launch. What I didn't bank on, was her taking such drastic measures to get a whole chapter to herself. Rest in peace Mum. It was the best of privileges and I'll miss you forever.

LEFT Julie and Mum.
Happy days.
ABOVE My brother André
wielding a berry picker.

Remember

Remember me when I am gone away,
Gone far away into the silent land;
When you can no more hold me by the hand,
Nor I half turn to go yet turning stay.
Remember me when no more day by day
You tell me of our future that you planned:
Only remember me; you understand
It will be late to counsel then or pray.
Yet if you should forget me for a while
And afterwards remember, do not grieve:
For if the darkness and corruption leave
A vestige of the thoughts that once I had,
Better by far you should forget and smile
Than that you should remember and be sad.

Christina Rossetti

Glossary of terms

Annual A plant that completes its life cycle in one year.

Bare root A tree or shrub sold without soil around its roots.

Biennial A plant that completes its life cycle over two years.

Biological control A means of pest control that relies on natural predatory or parasitic enemies.

Blanching A way of tenderising the flavour and texture of vegetables (typically celery, cardoon, chicory, leek, etc.) by excluding light from young shoots. Withholding light from a plant (e.g. rhubarb, celery) can make stems paler and sweeter. In the kitchen blanching refers to boiling briefly before immersing in cold water. This stops sugars being converted to starch and retains the integrity of the texture. Broad beans are usually blanched before freezing.

Bolting When a root or leaf vegetable begins to set seed. Once this occurs energy from the edible part of the crop is being used for seed production and the quality of the harvest is affected.

Blowing A term usually used for sprouts that are not tight in form. The leaves separate so that each sprout resembles a miniature cabbage. This loss of crunchiness makes them most unappealing.

Catch crop A fast-growing crop between plantings of main crops.

Cloche A miniature glazed structure to cover and protect vegetables during inclement weather.

Closed system Using only green manures and home-made compost to fertilise the soil.

Cordon A single-stem fruit tree planted at 45 degrees with side-shoots pruned to minimise the space it occupies.

Cotyledon The embryonic first leaves of a plant.

Cross-pollination When pollen is transferred from the anther (see Pollination) of one plant to the stigma of another.

Cut-and-come-again Leaf vegetables such as perpetual spinach (chard) and lettuce lend themselves to being harvested as they are growing. So long as the roots are in the ground, new leaves will grow as the plant is harvested. This is a particularly useful way of growing if you haven't got the hang of successional sowing.

Damping off A general term used for fungal diseases such as botrytis and phytophthora which kill seeds or seedlings. Overwatering, overcrowding and poor ventilation are the most common causes.

Dioecious Male and female flowers on separate plants (see Monoecious)

Earthing up Bringing soil up around the lower stem of a plant. A term usually used for potatoes, celery, leeks and sprouts.

Espalier A method of training trees to a flat plane where branches are tied onto a horizontal framework to control growth and make fit a specified shape. The

183

technique is often used as a decorative feature in formal designs, either free-standing or against walls and trellises.

FI hybrid Crossing two genetically different plants will produce an FI hybrid. This will carry inherent characteristics of each plant (e.g. better disease resistance, higher yield, etc.) at the expense of viable seed.

Family tree A fruit tree with more than one variety grafted to the main stem. A useful device for small gardens, guaranteeing pollination and extending the fruiting season.

Fan Like espaliers, a method of training trees to a flat plane where branches are tied onto a fan-shaped framework. The technique is usually applied to fruit of the prunus family.

Forcing Forcing plants usually means keeping them in a warmer protected environment where they will come into leaf more quickly. Forcing rhubarb, asparagus or chicory means also restricting light to encourage elongated stems that are more tender and sweet.

Hardening off Acclimatising slightly tender plants by subjecting them to somewhat cooler conditions (usually in a cold frame) before planting them outside.

Heeling in Planting temporarily, usually by laying a plant on its side in a trench and covering the roots with soil to stop them from drying out.

Lateral A branch that grows out from the main stem.

Leader The growing point of the main stem of a plant.

Ley crop A crop sown when soil is not being cropped for productive use to allow it to rejuvenate.

Maiden whip A one-year-old tree with no lateral shoots.

Monoecious Separate male and female flowers but carried on the same plant (see Dioecious).

Peak oil The period when the maximum rate of petroleum extraction is achieved worldwide and after which the rate of production diminishes in terminal decline.

Pernicious A term applied to plants that are invasive or so vigorous in habit that they can inhibit the growth of other plants and, in worst cases, threaten the natural habitat.

Perennial Plants, apart from woody trees and shrubs, that live for longer than two years. Herbaceous perennials are those plants that grow during spring and summer, die back and are dormant over winter, and then regrow from the rootstock the following season.

pH The measure used for the level of a soil's alkalinity or acidity. Soil with a pH value below 7.0 is more acidic while a higher reading than 7.0 indicates a more alkaline soil. Soil testing kits can be bought at most garden centres and are easy to use.

Pole See Rod.

Pollination The fertilisation of a plant when pollen is transferred from the stamen (the male part of a flower) to the stigma (the female part of a flower).

Potting on Replanting a plant that has outgrown its container.

Pricking out The transplanting of seedlings from a seed tray to a wider spacing in the ground or in a container.

Rod Also known as a pole or perch, a rod is a unit of length measuring 5.5 yards or 5.0292 metres. Despite decimalisation, allotments are still measured in rods or poles in the UK. Plots are typically referred to as being either five or ten rods, meaning five or ten square rods (approx. 125 or 250 square metres).

Rootstock A plant onto which a scion (see below) is grafted. The vigour of the rootstock (or stock) will dictate the eventual size of the plants.

Runner A stem growing from the base of a plant as an offset. Once sufficient roots have developed, it can be severed to make a new plant, as, for instance, strawberry.

Scion A twig or shoot with buds taken from the desired cultivar of a woody plant to be grafted onto the stock plant.

Self-fertile A plant that can pollinate itself and produce viable seed.

Sets Small, part-grown onion or shallot bulbs.

Sowing direct Sowing seeds directly into the soil.

Sowing under cover Sowing seeds under a cloche or in pots or modules inside a greenhouse or polytunnel.

Spur A short branched fruit-bearing shoot. Spurs can be encouraged on apple and pear trees by regular pruning.

Step-over A method of training fruit trees, similar to the espalier technique but with only one tier so that it can be stepped over. Commonly used as edging along paths and raised beds for kitchen gardens, the stunted growth prevents the tree from shading other vegetables.

Strig A cluster or string of currants.

Stockfree Farms that have no grazing animals and no animal input to any part of the growing process.

Successional sowing Spacing sowing times to avoid having a glut of any particular vegetable at any given time.

Sucker Someone who takes on an allotment or … A new stem or stems growing from the rootstock part of a grafted plant. These should be removed to direct all the plant's energy to the grafted cultivar.

Tilth Tilth is nothing short of horticultural nirvana, being friable soil that has an optimal level of sand, clay and organic matter making it ideal for growing seeds in. 'Rake to a good tilth' is the most common expression but something that can take years to achieve on heavy soil.

Top dressing A layer of compost (mulch) or quick-acting fertiliser on the soil surface. An autumn layer of well-rotted compost or farmyard manure will help feed the soil, suppress weeds and protect bare patches from erosion during the winter months.

Book list and websites

Here is a list of books, suppliers and websites that I've found very useful over the years.
The ones with recipes are always close to hand and are marked with an asterisk.

Arrigo, Paolo, *From Seed to Plate*, Simon & Schuster Ltd.,
    London, 2009*

Biggs, Tony, *RHS Growing Vegetables*, Mitchell Beazley, London,
    1999

Clifford, King, Ravillious et al., *The Common Ground Book of
    Orchards*, Common Ground Publishing, London, 2000

Deakin, Roger, *Notes from Walnut Tree Farm*, Hamish
    Hamilton, London, 2008

Diacono, Mark, *Veg Patch*, Bloomsbury, London, 2009*

— *A Taste of the Unexpected*. Quadrille, London, 2008

Don, Monty and Sarah, *Fork to Fork*, Conran Octopus,
    London, 1999*

Dowding, Charles, *Organic Gardening: The Natural No-Dig Way*,
    Green Books, Totnes, 2007*

Hall, Jenny and Iain Tolhurst, *Growing Green*, Vegan Organic
    Network, Altrincham, 2006

Heinberg, Richard, *The Party's Over: Oil, war and the fate of
    industrial societies*, Clairview Books, Forest Row, 2003

Hessayon, Dr D. G., *The Vegetable and Herb Expert*, Expert, 2nd
    revised edition 1997

Hills, Lawrence D., *Fertility Gardening*, David & Charles,
    London, 1981

Klein, Carol, *Grow Your Own Veg*, Mitchell Beazley, London,
    2007

Kollerstrom, Nick, *Gardening and Planting by the Moon*,
    Quantum/Foulsham, Slough, 2004

Larkcom, Joy, *Grow Your Own Vegetables*, Frances Lincoln,
    London, 2002

Leendertz, Lia, *The Half Hour Allotment*, Frances Lincoln,
    London, 2006

Lloyd, Christopher, *Gardener Cook*, Frances Lincoln, London,
    1997*

McVicar, Jekka, *Jekka's Complete Herb Book*, Kyle Cathie,
    London, 2009

Pears, Pauline and Sue Stickland, *RHS Organic Gardening*,
    Mitchell Beazley, London, 1995

Roberts, Juliet, *Organic Kitchen Garden*, Conran Octopus,
    London, 2005

Stickland, Sue, *Back Garden Seed Saving: Keeping our vegetable
    heritage alive*, Eco-Logic Books/Worldly Goods, Bath,
    2008

Thompson, Ken, *Compost: The natural way to make food for your
    garden*, Dorling Kindersley, London, 2007

Thompson, Ken, *No Nettles Required*, Transworld, London,
    2007

Thun, Maria and Matthias, *The Biodynamic Sowing and Planting
    Calendar*, Floris Books, Edinburgh, published annually

Seed and seedling suppliers

Delfland Nurseries, www.rocketgardens.co.uk

Green Manure Seeds, www.greenmanure.co.uk

The Heritage Seed Library, www.gardenorganic.org.uk/hsl

Jekka's herb Farm, www.jekkasherbfarm.co.uk

The Organic Gardening Catalogue, www.organiccatalog.com

The Real Seed Company, www.realseeds.co.uk

Rocket Gardens, www.rocketgardens.co.uk

Suffolk Herbs, www.suffolkherbs.com

Thomas Etty, www.thomasetty.co.uk

Useful websites

www.biodynamic.org.uk

www.gardenorganic.co.uk

www.landshare.net (linking people who want to grow food
    to land on which to grow it)

www.rhs.org.uk

www.seedtoplate.co.uk (planting calendar, design a plot
    online, video guides, seeds etc.)

www.soilassociation.org.uk

www.tolhurstorganic.co.uk

A not very useful website

www.3menwent2mow.com

Index
Numbers in *italic* refer to illustrations

Acknowledgements

As this book has turned out to be something of a personal reflection I'd like to go a little over the top here, just in case I never write another.

I should first of all thank the team at Frances Lincoln, and in particular, Jane Crawley and Andrew Dunn for giving me the chance to write this the way I saw it, Nancy Marten for essential proofreading and Becky Clarke for capturing the spirit of our plot. Thanks also to my cousin, Derek St Romaine for his support over the years, the photographs for this book and his generosity in allowing me to express myself with my own. My dad, Vic West, deserves a medal for his patience with indexing and I'd like to extend my appreciation to my agent, Lina Costanza, for her patience and support over the years while searching for the right publisher. It's been a long road.

My gratitude also extends to the following people, not necessarily involved with the book itself, but whose influence and support have helped me find a path that I didn't know I had the right shoes for.

Dick and Kit Boustead for your teaching and guidance in the early years. Elsie Ivy Sampson, Anne West and Alun Jenkins for sowing the first seeds. Terry Torpey for your wisdom and counsel at the crossroads. Pat Smart and Keith for giving me a chance when I knew nothing at all. Mr and Mrs A. W. Hector, ditto and for showing the value of taking one's time. Ted Hylands for your patience when teaching me about bricks and slabs and keeping me in work when times were hard. Rod Woodruff for your help and encouragement when our sporting careers spluttered and died. Sculptor, Johnny Woodford for your friendship, collaborations and lateral take on the world. John Brookes for your wisdom and teaching – what a privilege that was! Phil Nash for introducing me to Bushy Park Allotment Association and Jackie Dungate, our then allotment officer, who tempted us to take on more then we could chew. Victoria Summerly for your confidence in introducing me to the *Independent Magazine*. Anna Pavord for your enthusiasm and encouragement during a fun five years as your sidekick. Ian Hodgson and Juliet Roberts who saw the mileage in allotments. My assistant, Humaira Ikram, for your vitality and patience in a very random office. Chris and Toby Marchant, unsung heroes of my (and many other) show gardens, for your friendship, love and counsel. Agnes and Serge Bottagisio-Decoux for fruitful collaborations. Camilla and Jeremy Swift and Jekka McVicar for your love, help and encouragement, especially during crises of confidence. Mark Diacono for inspiring us enough to (maybe) give it another ten years, and not forgetting Joe Swift, James Alexander-Sinclair (my support act in 'Three Men Went to Mow' who will only sulk if they don't get a mention), Ann-Marie Powell, Annie Guilfoyle (and The Garden Monkey) for reminding us not to take ourselves too seriously.

And at the allotment . . .

Giuseppe for bringing the shop back from the brink and for your calm. Henry for your optimism, sense of justice and for standing up for the vulnerable. Sainsbury's John for your kindness, sense of humour and generosity. John Whitby for keeping us all watered. Kathy for being a lovely neighbour. Mary for your help and watchfulness. David and Julie for your affection and help over the years through thick and thin. Chi and family for your inspiration and advice. Phil Iddison for providing the benchmark that we all aspire to and for your commitment in helping Bushy Park Allotment Association achieve its potential. Ralph and Julia for your kindness. Rick for keeping the flag of eccentricity flying high. Ted Leopard for your continuous support, generosity and laughs. Dhundi Raj, Natasha, East and Phulmaya. . . wish you were still here.

And finally . . .

Simon Sales and Paul Cossell for your friendship, help and moral support, especially when watching Brentford FC. Phil Barthropp for being there, whenever, whatever, wherever. Dad for keeping the faith when I chose gardening as a career and for your wonderful Victor Meldrew moments. My brother André and my aunt Jacqui for your love and support when our world caved in. Mum and Larry for all your hard work while we were away from our plot, and for your love, devotion and laughter that knew no bounds. Thank you too, Joan Kirkpatrick, for more than you'll ever know. Last and by no means least, Christine. There aren't enough Gold Medals in the world for your love, patience, strength and optimism.

I'm a lone ranger, so I don't grow vegetables for myself but I eat lots of them – even my 5 a day, and so I applaud their cultivators. And I enjoy sharing the fruits of their labour too and readily agree their beaming 'Aren't these delicious, so much tastier than bought?' and I think to myself 'Are they'? Cabbage is cabbage surely, and frozen peas they tell me are even fresher than home grown. The secret I believed is how you cook and present your veg. So I'm a great believer in Fork to Fork. And I do understand the thrill of growing your own, it's truly an achievement!

But what I really commend is the down-to-earthiness of the veg grower – and there are many more than allotment holders only.

As a landscape designer (who incidentally taught your author at a design school at Kew, and he was good) it worries me the diminishing numbers of people who get their hands dirty in good earth. Increasingly generations are now urban dwellers and are all too often represented by garden journalists who wouldn't dream of getting muddy, and their country experience is limited to properties open for charity in the Yellow Book.

Yet kids are taught ecology, they go hiking and go for farm and country visits nowadays, so where does it all go astray?

Well, perhaps I'm wrong and it doesn't. At a later stage in their lives they all have gardens and/or allotments, and if they are between jobs or 'resting' have time to work them too! For, as Cleve points out, veg growing is almost a life style. I presumably have missed out on the bonhomie of the allotment I fear, as I weed my garden in solitary silence. I must be strange, since it is that contemplative quiet exercise which I love, surrounded by growing things – just the wrong type perhaps!.

John Brookes MBE

In this book Cleve beautifully illustrates the successes and the failures, the camaraderie and the generosity of the fellow gardener; and how, despite worldly pressures on the environment, the food chain and green space, the gardener is the eternal optimist – for there is always next year.

Jekka McVicar

You know that line we all trot out – 'Growing your own delicious food is easy, anyone can do it . . .', well, here's proof at last: if Cleve can, rest assured, anyone can. And he does it very beautifully. Not him, I mean his allotment. Which is not to say he's not good looking . . . not that I find him good looking personally although objectively I can see he's not ugly.

Mark Diacono at Otter Farm

Allotment envy or what? Not only has Cleve got umpteen Gold Medals at Chelsea, but he's also got the best allotment I've ever seen. He practically lives on it during spring and summer. It's the perfect place to escape and fortunately I get the odd invite but isn't 4 sheds going too far?

Joe Swift

Until I met Cleve I thought that allotmenteering was something you did on a mountain with a compass and a pair of sturdy boots. Having visited his plot I now know that it is something more satisfying, less windswept and (above all) much more delicious. You still need the boots though.

James Alexander-Sinclair